TRUTH AND ERROR

Zondervan
Guide to Cults &
Religious Movements

Truth and Error
Copyright © 1998 by Alan W. Gomes

Requests for information should be addressed to:

ZondervanPublishingHouse
Grand Rapids, Michigan 49530

Library of Congress Cataloging-in-Publication Data

Gomes, Alan W., 1955–
   Truth and error : comparative charts of cults and Christianity / Alan W. Gomes.
      p.   cm. — (Zondervan guide to cults & religious movements)
     ISBN 0-310-22049-1
     1. Religions—Controversial literature—Charts, diagrams, etc. 2. Cults—
Controversial literature—Charts, diagrams, etc. I. Title. II. Series.
   BL85.G64   1998
   261.2—dc21   97-48797
                                                          CIP

Interior design by Art Jacobs

Printed in the United States of America

98 99 00 01 02 03 04 05 /❖ DP/ 10 9 8 7 6 5 4 3 2 1

Contents

 Preface

The *Zondervan Guide to Cults and Religious Movements* comprises fifteen volumes, treating some of the most important groups and belief systems confronting the Christian church today. Written in the form of a detailed outline, this series distills the most important facts about each and presents a well-reasoned, cogent Christian response. Each volume is written by a recognized expert or experts on the topic and presents a fair, accurate, and well-documented presentation of the group's beliefs and teachings. Each group is then critiqued from a biblical Christian perspective.

One of the most helpful features is the parallel comparison chart that appears at the end of most of the volumes. Arranged topically, the chart juxtaposes direct quotations from the group's literature in the left column with a biblical refutation on the right. The group's quotations are properly referenced, enabling one to go directly to the source for further study.

The chart is very useful in a couple of different ways. First, it serves as a virtual summary of the entire book. For someone who has read the book and has studied the detailed discussion, the chart provides a handy review. For someone who has not yet read the book or does not have the time to study it in detail, the chart gives a good overall idea of what each group teaches and provides biblical arguments to counter those beliefs. Another important use is in an actual witnessing situation. Because the chart presents unaltered word-for-word quotations directly from the group's own literature—including the complete reference as to where these words may be found—the quotations can provide the basis for witnessing dialogue. The solid biblical arguments against the ideas expressed in each quote—also properly referenced—assist in sharing the truth. The topical arrangement makes it easy to find relevant material quickly, as would be needed in an impromptu situation.

Because of their value, all these charts have been collected into the present volume to form a handy, stand-alone reference. To introduce them is a brief overview of each group's history and belief system. These short overviews provide some context for the quotations that appear in the parallel charts. Anyone wanting more detailed information should consult the complete book on the topic.

Two books in the series do not contain parallel charts. Instead, an overview of these books appears at the end of this volume, in which the main arguments and issues contained in the book are summarized.

We hope that you will find this book to be a handy tool as you seek to give reasons for your faith (1 Peter 3:15).

—Alan W. Gomes

# Chapter I
Jehovah's Witnesses

Author: Robert M. Bowman, Jr.; summary by Alan W. Gomes

Background

The Watchtower Bible and Tract Society, more commonly known as Jehovah's Witnesses, was founded in the 1880s by Charles Taze Russell, a haberdasher from Allegheny, Pennsylvania. Russell, who attended Presbyterian and Congregational churches as a child, found himself unable to accept their teaching about hell. Under Seventh-day Adventist influence, Russell embraced their teaching that "hell" stood for the grave and that the wicked would ultimately be annihilated, not tortured consciously for eternity. Also through Adventist influence, Russell adopted the idea that Christ's second coming was an invisible, spiritual "presence" that had already begun, rather than a literal, bodily return to take place in the future. Russell also denied the doctrines of the Trinity and of Christ's deity. He was known for his vociferous denunciations of "Christendom's" allegedly false beliefs and practices. Russell died in 1916, believing that World War I was Armageddon.

Joseph Franklin Rutherford (d. 1942), the society's legal counselor, succeeded Russell as head of the movement, and it was under his tenure that they adopted the name "Jehovah's Witnesses." The current Watchtower president is Milton G. Henschel. In terms of social and ethical practices, JWs do not observe birthdays, Christmas, Easter, Thanksgiving, Mother's Day, or any other such holidays, rejecting them as "pagan." They refuse blood transfusions (based on a misunderstanding of Leviticus 17), will not participate in politics or the military, and will not salute the flag. They maintain strict neutrality in war. There are presently at least 5 million active JWs worldwide. They are known for their massive proselytizing efforts, dedicating about one billion hours per year to witnessing (that is, over 200 hours per member per year). JWs also distribute enormous amounts of printed literature, more so than any other cult.

Summary of Beliefs

Jehovah's Witnesses believe that there is one almighty **God** by nature, who is also only one person. JWs wrongly allege that wicked scribes removed God's proper name, Jehovah, from the Bible. This divine name has been restored to its rightful place in the New World Translation of the Bible. The doctrine of the **Trinity** is roundly condemned as unscriptural and the result of pagan influences. **Jesus Christ** was Michael the Archangel before his incarnation as a man; after

7

his death and spiritual resurrection (see below), the man Jesus again became an angel. Jesus was Jehovah's agent in creating all things after he himself was created by Jehovah God. Although not God by nature, he is a "mighty one" and therefore may be called "a god" in a loose sense of the word. The **Holy Spirit** is not a person, nor a member of the Godhead, but is Jehovah's active force, which emanates from him to accomplish his will.

Concerning the **afterlife,** Jehovah's Witnesses do not believe in an entity called the soul that survives the death of the body. Rather, they teach that people cease to exist at death but that at the Resurrection Jehovah will recreate them from his memory. In the eternal state there are different classes of Christians with different destinies. The **144,000** are those who, along with Christ Jesus, are "born again" to exist as spirits; they will reign with Christ in heaven. The rest will live in a paradise earth with resurrected bodies. There is no **hell** in the traditional understanding of the doctrine; the finally impenitent will be annihilated, not tortured for all eternity.

Concerning **Christ's death and resurrection,** he gave his life as a ransom price to atone for our guilt in Adam. He was raised an invisible spirit creature, forfeiting his right to bodily, earthly life. **Salvation** is accomplished by faith in Christ Jesus plus works, such as taking in spiritual knowledge and doing God's kingdom work (such as door-to-door witnessing). Regarding **Christ's second coming,** JWs reject the notion that Christ will return bodily to earth. Rather, his invisible "presence," which began in 1914, is engineering events leading to the Battle of Armageddon and the beginning of the Millennium. The Watchtower Society is known for having set several different dates for when Armageddon would occur; after each failed prophecy, numerous disillusioned members left the movement.

Parallel Comparison Chart

Jehovah's Witnesses	The Bible
Scripture and Watchtower Authority	
"They say that it is sufficient to read the Bible exclusively, either alone or in small groups at home. But, strangely, through such 'Bible reading,' they have reverted right back to the apostate doctrines that commentaries by Christendom's clergy were teaching 100 years ago . . ." (*The Watchtower*, August 15, 1981, 28–29).	"All Scripture is inspired of God and beneficial for teaching, for reproving, for setting things straight, for disciplining in righteousness, that the man of God may be *fully competent, completely equipped* for every good work" (2 Tim. 3:16–17 NWT).[*]
	"I am writing these things to you about those who are trying to lead you astray.

---

[*]Note: All italics in quotations in this chart are added for emphasis unless otherwise noted.

As for you, the anointing you received from him remains in you, and you do not need anyone to teach you. But as his anointing teaches you about all things and as that anointing is real, not counterfeit—just as it has taught you, remain in him" (1 John 2:26–27 NIV).

The Deity of Christ

"... the Bible plainly states that in his prehuman existence, Jesus was a created spirit being, just as angels were spirit beings created by God.... The fact is that Jesus is not God and never claimed to be" (*Should You Believe in the Trinity?* [1989], 14, 20).

"In the beginning was the Word, and the Word was with God, and the Word was God" (John 1:1 NIV).

"'I tell you the truth,' Jesus answered, 'before Abraham was born, I am!'" (John 8:58 NIV).

"In answer Thomas said to him [Jesus]: 'My Lord and my God!'" (John 20:28 NWT).

"So it was by means of this master worker, his junior partner, as it were, that Almighty God created all other things.... he was simply addressing another individual, his first spirit creation, the master craftsman, the prehuman Jesus" (*Should You Believe in the Trinity?* 14).

"I, Jehovah, am doing everything, stretching out the heavens by myself, laying out the earth. Who was with me?" (Is. 44:24 NWT).

"All things came into existence through him, and apart from him not even one thing came into existence" (John 1:3 NWT).

The Personhood of the Holy Spirit

"The correct identification of the holy spirit must fit *all the scriptures* that refer to that spirit. With this viewpoint, it is logical to conclude that the holy spirit is the active force of God. It is not a person but is a powerful force that God causes to emanate from himself to accomplish his holy will" (*Reasoning from the Scriptures* [1985], 381).

"However, when that one *arrives*, the spirit of the truth, he will *guide* YOU into all the truth, for he will not *speak* on *his own impulse*, but what things he *hears* he will speak, and he will *declare* to YOU the things coming. That one will *glorify* me, because he will *receive* from what is mine and will *declare it* to YOU" (John 16:13–14 NWT).

9

Death

"At death man's spirit, his life-force, which is sustained by breathing, 'goes out.' *It no longer exists....* When they are dead, both humans and animals are in this same state of complete unconsciousness.... That the soul lives on after death is a lie started by the Devil" (*You Can Live Forever in Paradise on Earth* [1982], 77).

"You have come to God, the judge of all men, to *the spirits* of righteous men made perfect" (Heb. 12:23 NIV).

"... I saw underneath the altar the souls of those who had been slaughtered because of the word of God and because of the witness work that they used to have. And they cried with a loud voice, saying ..." (Rev. 6:9–10 NWT).

Hell

"Would a *loving God* really torment people forever? ... The wicked, of course, are not literally tormented because, as we have seen, when a person is dead he is completely out of existence.... And it is also a lie, which the Devil spread, that the souls of the wicked are tormented..." (*You Can Live Forever in Paradise on Earth*, 81, 88, 89).

"Actually, all this passage [Rev. 14:9–11] says is that the wicked are tormented, not that they are tormented forever. The text says that it is the *smoke* ... that continues forever, not the fiery torment" ("Hell—Eternal Torture or Common Grave?" *The Watchtower*, April 15, 1993, 7).

"If anyone worships the wild beast and its image ... he will also drink of the wine of the *anger of God* that is poured out undiluted into the cup of *his wrath*, and *he shall be tormented* with fire and sulphur in the sight of the holy angels and in the sight of the Lamb. And the smoke of their torment ascends forever and ever, and day and night *they have no rest....* And the Devil who was misleading them was hurled into the lake of fire and sulphur, where both the wild beast and the false prophet [already were]; and *they will be tormented day and night forever and ever*" (Rev. 14:9–11; 20:10 NWT).

Christ's Death

"Jehovah God has the right to refuse to accept a ransom for anyone he deems unworthy. Christ's ransom covers the sins an individual has because of being a child of Adam, but a person can add to that by his own, deliberate, willful course of action, and he can thus die for such sin that is beyond coverage by the ransom" (*Insight on the Scriptures* [1988], 2:792).

"... for *all* have sinned and fall short of the glory of God, and are justified freely by his grace through the redemption that came by Christ Jesus" (Rom. 3:23–24 NIV).

"You see, at just the right time, when we were still powerless, Christ died for the ungodly" (Rom. 5:6 NIV).

"Christ Jesus came into the world to save sinners—of whom I am *the worst*" (1 Tim. 1:15 NIV).

"The blood of Jesus . . . cleanses us from *all* sin" (1 John 1:7 NWT).

Christ's Resurrection

"Having given up his flesh for the life of the world, Christ could never take it again and become a man once more. For that basic reason his return could never be in the human body that he sacrificed once for all time" (*You Can Live Forever in Paradise on Earth*, 143).

"But God resurrected him by loosing the pangs of death, because it was not possible for him to continue to be held fast by it. For David says respecting him . . . 'On this account my heart became cheerful and my tongue rejoiced greatly. Moreover, even my *flesh* will reside in hope . . .'" (Acts 2:24–27 NWT).

Classes of Christians

"So this 'congregation of God' is made up of all Christians on earth who have the hope of heavenly life. In all, only 144,000 persons finally make up the 'congregation of God.' Today, only a few of these, a remnant, are still on earth. Christians who hope to live forever on earth look for spiritual guidance from members of this 'congregation of the living God'" (*You Can Live Forever in Paradise on Earth*, 125–26).

"For truly by one spirit we were *all* baptized into *one body* ..." (1 Cor. 12:13 NWT).

"... you were slain, and with your blood you purchased men for God from every tribe and language and people and nation. You have made them to be a kingdom and priests to serve our God, and they will reign *on the earth*" (Rev. 5:9–10 NIV).

The New Birth

"Being born again involves being baptized in water ('born from water') and begotten by God's spirit ('born from . . . spirit'), thus becoming a son of God with the prospect of sharing in the Kingdom of God. (John 3:3–5) Jesus had this experience, as do the 144,000 who are heirs with him of the heavenly Kingdom" (*Reasoning from the Scriptures*, 76).

"For *all* who are led by God's spirit, these are God's sons" (Rom. 8:14 NWT).

"You are *all* sons of God through faith in Christ Jesus" (Gal. 3:26 NIV).

"*Everyone* believing that Jesus is the Christ has been born from God" (1 John 5:1 NWT).

11

Salvation

"Some suggest that belief in Jesus is the end of the matter.... However, to concentrate on only one essential requirement for salvation to the exclusion of the others is like reading one crucial clause in a contract and ignoring the rest.... Yes, there are various things involved in getting saved. We must take in accurate knowledge of God's purposes and his way of salvation. Then we must exercise faith in the Chief Agent of salvation, Jesus Christ, and do God's will the rest of our lives. (John 3:16; Titus 2:14)" ("What We Must Do to Be Saved," *The Watchtower*, September 15, 1993, 5–7).

"For God so loved the world that he gave his one and only Son, that whoever believes in him shall not perish but have eternal life" (John 3:16–18 NIV).

"For it is by grace you have been saved, through faith—and this not from yourselves, it is the gift of God—not by works, so that no one can boast. For we are God's workmanship, created in Christ Jesus to do good works, which God prepared in advance for us to do" (Eph. 2:8–10 NIV).

"... our great God and Savior, Jesus Christ, who gave himself for us to redeem us from all wickedness and to purify for himself a people that are his very own, eager to do what is good.... But when the kindness and love of God our Savior appeared, he saved us, not because of righteous things we had done, but because of his mercy" (Titus 2:13–14; 3:4–5 NIV).

Christ's Return

"For some 79 years, humans on earth have been experiencing the effects of Christ's invisible royal presence" ("Shedding Light on Christ's Presence," *The Watchtower*, May 1, 1993, 11).

"For the Lord himself will come down from heaven, with a loud command, with the voice of the archangel and with the trumpet call of God, and the dead in Christ will rise first" (1 Thess. 4:16 NIV).

Sources

Insight on the Scriptures, 2 vols. (Brooklyn: Watchtower Bible and Tract Society of New York, Inc., 1988).

New World Translation of the Holy Scriptures: With References, rev. ed. (Brooklyn: Watchtower Bible and Tract Society of New York, Inc., 1984).

Reasoning from the Scriptures (Brooklyn: Watchtower Bible and Tract Society of New York, Inc., 1985).

Should You Believe in the Trinity? (Brooklyn: Watchtower Bible and Tract Society of New York, Inc., 1989).

You Can Live Forever in Paradise on Earth (Brooklyn: Watchtower Bible and Tract Society of New York, Inc., 1982).

 # Chapter II:
Mormonism

Author: Kurt Van Gorden; summary by Alan W. Gomes

Background

The Church of Jesus Christ of Latter-day Saints, more commonly known as the Mormon Church, was founded by Joseph Smith, Jr. (1805–44), a resident of upstate New York. Smith claimed that God the Father and Jesus Christ appeared to him in 1820, informing him that all the churches were wrong, their creeds an abomination, and their professors corrupt. In 1823 an angel named Moroni appeared to him, telling him of golden plates that were buried in a nearby hillside. These plates allegedly contained a record of ancient peoples who had migrated from the Near East to America. In 1827 Moroni directed Smith to unearth the plates and begin, with supernatural help, "translating" the "Reformed Egyptian hieroglyphic" characters allegedly inscribed on them. In March 1830, Smith published the resulting "Book of Mormon," purported to contain the "fullness of the gospel," and founded his church one month later.

After Smith's demise at the hands of an angry mob (1844), Brigham Young (1801–77) took over leadership of the group, relocating the "Saints" to Utah. The current Mormon prophet is Gordon B. Hinckley. Today, the Mormon church boasts a worldwide membership of around 10 million. Mormons actively engage in missionary outreach and literature distribution. Financially prosperous, they are second only to the Roman Catholic Church in total wealth. Mormons are often known for their emphasis on "family values" and a clean-cut lifestyle.

Summary of Beliefs

One fundamental difference between Mormonism and orthodox Christianity is that Mormonism is polytheistic, while Christianity is strictly monotheistic. Concerning **God,** Mormons believe in an eternal progression of gods begetting other gods. "God the Father" is one such god, and he is the god over this planet—the god "with whom we have to do." However, it is also true that God the Father is a man, who attained exaltation to godhood by obedience to the same gospel principles that Mormons strive to obey. God the Father has a body of flesh and bones as tangible as ours. Mormons deny the biblical doctrine of the **Trinity,** teaching that Father, Son, and Holy Ghost are three separate gods.

Concerning **man,** Mormons teach that he is a god "in embryo" and may attain exaltation to godhood as his heavenly father has. God and man are of the same "species," the former being an exalted and glorified instance of the latter.

13

Before their birth into this present world, all human beings preexisted in heaven as spiritual progeny of a father and mother god/goddess. They have no memory of their previous existence in the spirit realm. If sufficiently obedient to Mormon teaching and certain practices, they will achieve exaltation. Those exalted will inhabit a planet and procreate spirit children, continuing the aforementioned cycle. Concerning **Jesus Christ,** Mormons teach that he is Lucifer's spirit brother because they were procreated by the same parents (that is, in his preexistent state, before his incarnation). They deny the virgin birth, teaching instead that the human body of Jesus was the product of actual sexual intercourse between God the Father and Mary. (Remember that the Father is a man with a physical body.)

Concerning **salvation,** Mormons deny the biblical doctrine of salvation by grace, teaching instead that we can attain salvation through "repentance, baptism, faith, and good works." Christ's atoning work brings about the resurrection of all mankind, but it cannot pay for all a person's sins or guarantee exaltation. While Christ's work is the beginning of salvation, human works are needed to complete the process. Depending on those works, people will achieve one of three levels of heaven: the telestial, the terrestrial, or the celestial. Temple marriage is required for one to attain the celestial kingdom, the highest level.

Parallel Comparison Chart

Mormonism	The Bible
Continued Revelation	
"The canon of scripture is not full. God has never revealed at any time that he would cease to speak forever to men" (*Gospel Doctrine*, 36).	"From Jerusalem all the way around to Illyricum, I *have fully proclaimed the gospel* of Christ" (Rom. 15:19).
"Modern revelation is necessary. . . . If we are permitted to believe that he has spoken, we must and do believe that he continues to speak, because he is unchangeable" (*Gospel Doctrine*, 36).	"I felt I had to write and urge you to contend for *the faith that was once for all entrusted* to the saints" (Jude 3).
The Creator	
"The Gods organized and formed the heavens and earth. . . . And they (the Gods) said: Let there be light; and there was light. And they (the Gods) comprehended the light. . . . And the Gods called	"In the beginning God created the heavens and the earth" (Gen. 1:1). "You alone are the LORD. You made the heavens, even the highest heavens, and

the light Day" (Pearl of Great Price, Book of Abraham, 4:1–5).

"In the beginning the head of the Gods called a council of the Gods; and they came together and concocted a plan to create and populate the world and people it" (*Journal of Discourses*, 6:5).

all their starry host, the earth and all that is on it, the seas and all that is in them. You give life to everything, and the multitudes of heaven worship you" (Neh. 9:6).

The Uniqueness of God

"I will preach on the plurality of Gods. . . . I wish to declare I have always and in all congregations, when I have preached on the subject of Deity, it has been the plurality of Gods" (*Documentary History of the Church*, 6:474).

"We have imagined and supposed that God was God from all eternity. I will refute that idea, and take away the veil, so that you can see" (*Documentary History of the Church*, 6:304).

"Hear, O Israel: The LORD our God, the LORD is one" (Deut. 6:4).

"Before me no god was formed, nor will there be one after me" (Isa. 43:10).

"Apart from me there is no God" (Isa. 44:6).

The Trinity

"Many men say there is one God; the Father, the Son, and the Holy Ghost are only one God! I say that this is a strange God anyhow—three in one, and one in three!... He would be a wonderfully big God—He would be a giant or a monster" (*Documentary History of the Church*, 6:476).

"This revealed doctrine of the composition and nature of the Godhead teaches that there are at least three Gods" (*Evidences and Reconciliation*, 65).

"Hear, O Israel: The LORD our God, the LORD is one" (Deut. 6:4).

"Go and make disciples of all nations, baptizing them in the name of the Father and of the Son and of the Holy Spirit" (Matt. 28:19).

There are different kinds of worship, but *the same God*" (1 Cor. 12:4–6, emphasis added).

The Nature of God the Father

"First, God himself, who sits enthroned in yonder heavens, is a man like unto one of yourselves" (*Times and Seasons*, 5:613).

"The Father has a body of flesh and bones as tangible as man's" (Doctrine and Covenants, 130:22).

"For I am God, and not man—the Holy One among you" (Hos. 11:9).

"God is spirit" (John 4:24).

"A spirit hath not flesh and bones" (Luke 24:39 KJV).

The Virgin Birth of Jesus Christ

"When the virgin Mary conceived the child Jesus, the Father had begotten him in his own likeness. He was not begotten by the Holy Ghost.... Now remember from this time forth, and forever, that Jesus Christ was not begotten by the Holy Ghost" (*Journal of Discourses*, 1:50–51).

"The body in which He performed His mission in the flesh was sired by that same Holy Being we worship as God, our Eternal Father" (*Teachings of the Prophet Ezra Taft Benson*, 7).

"She [Mary] was found to be with child through the Holy Spirit" (Matt. 1:18).

"'How will this be,' Mary asked the angel, 'since I am a virgin?'" (Luke 1:34).

"The Holy Spirit will come upon you [Mary], and the power of the Most High will overshadow you" (Luke 1:35).

The Atonement of Jesus Christ

"It is true that the blood of the Son of God was shed for sins through the fall and those committed by men, yet men can commit sins which it can never remit" (*Journal of Discourses*, 4:59).

"Joseph Smith taught that there were certain sins so grievous that man may commit, that they will place the transgressors beyond the power of the atonement of Christ" (*Doctrines of Salvation*, 1:138).

"The blood of Christ will never wipe that out, your own blood must atone for it" (*Journal of Discourses*, 3:247).

"If we walk in the light, as he is in the light, we have fellowship with one another, and the blood of Jesus, his Son, purifies us from *all* sin" (1 John 1:7).

"To him who loves us and has freed us from our sins by his blood" (Rev. 1:5).

"So Christ was sacrificed once to take away the sins of many people" (Heb. 9:28).

The Holy Spirit

"The Holy Ghost is the third member of the Godhead. He is a Personage of Spirit, a Spirit Person, a *Spirit Man*, a Spirit Entity. He can be in only one place at one time and he does not and cannot transform himself into any other form or image than that of the *Man whom he is*" (*Mormon Doctrine*, 358 [emphasis added]).

"You have lied to the Holy Spirit.... You have not lied to men but to God" (Acts 5:3–4).

"Where can I go from your Spirit? Where can I flee from your presence? If I go up to the heavens, you are there; if I make my bed in the depths, you are there" (Ps. 139:7–8).

Human Nature

"You have got to learn how to be gods yourselves, and to be kings and priests to God, the same as all gods have done before you" (*Documentary History of the Church*, 6:306).

"Then shall they be gods, because they have no end.... Then shall they be gods. ...Abraham... Isaac... and Jacob... are not angels but are gods" (Doctrine and Covenants, 132:20, 37).

"Moses replied, 'It will be as you say, so that you may know there is no one like the LORD our God'" (Ex. 8:10).

"How great you are, O Sovereign LORD! There is no one like you, and there is no God but you" (2 Sam. 7:22).

"I am God, and not man—the Holy One among you" (Hosea 11:9).

Sin

"Divine justice forbids that we be accounted sinners solely because our parents transgressed" (Talmage, *Articles of Faith*, 475).

"We believe that men will be punished for their own sins, and not for Adam's transgression" (Articles of Faith, 2).

"Therefore, just as sin entered the world through man [Adam], and death through sin, and in this way death came to all men, because all sinned" (Rom. 5:12).

"Through the disobedience of the one man [Adam] the many were made sinners" (Rom. 5:19).

Salvation

"Full salvation is attained by virtue of knowledge, truth, righteousness, and all true principles. Many conditions must exist in order to make such salvation available to men. Without continuous revelation, the ministering of angels, the working of miracles, the prevalence of gifts of the spirit, there would be no salvation. There is no salvation outside the Church of Jesus Christ of Latter-day Saints" (*Mormon Doctrine*, 670).

"It is by grace you have been saved, through faith—and this not from yourselves, it is the gift of God—not by works, so that no one can boast" (Eph. 2:8–9).

"He saved us, not because of righteous things we had done, but because of his mercy" (Titus 3:5).

Eternal Retribution

"Those who live lives of wickedness may also be heirs of salvation, that is, they too shall be redeemed from death and from hell eventually. These, however, must suffer in hell the torments of the damned until they pay the price of their sinning, for the blood of Christ will not cleanse them" (*Doctrines of Salvation*, 2:133–34).

"Then they [those who do not follow Christ] will go away to *eternal* punishment" (Matt. 25:46).

"It is better for you to enter life maimed than with two hands to go into hell, where the fire never goes out" (Mark 9:43).

Sources

Ezra Taft Benson, *Teachings of the Prophet Ezra Taft Benson* (Salt Lake City: Bookcraft, 1988).

Bruce R. McConkie, *Mormon Doctrine* (Salt Lake City: Bookcraft, 1966).

F. D. Richards, comp., *Journal of Discourses,* 26 vols. (Liverpool: Latter-day Saint Book Depot, 1855–1886).

Joseph Smith Jr., The Doctrine and Covenants (Kirtland, Ohio: 1835; rev. ed., Salt Lake City: Corporation of the Church of Jesus Christ of Latter-day Saints, 1981).

Joseph Smith Jr., *Doctrines of Salvation,* 3 vols. (Salt Lake City: Bookcraft, 1959).

Joseph Smith Jr., *Documented History of the Church of Jesus Christ of Latter-day Saints,* 6 vols., ed. B. H. Roberts (Salt Lake City: Deseret Book Co., 1978).

Joseph Smith Jr., Pearl of Great Price (Liverpool: 1851; rev. ed., Salt Lake City: The Church of Jesus Christ of Latter-day Saints, 1981).

Joseph Smith Jr., *Times and Seasons,* 6 vols. (Nauvoo, Ill.: The Church of Jesus Christ of Latter-day Saints, n.d.).

Joseph F. Smith, *Gospel Doctrine* (Salt Lake City: Deseret Book Co., 1977).

James E. Talmage, *Articles of Faith* (Salt Lake City: Deseret Book Co., 1981).

John A. Widtsoe, *Evidences and Reconciliation* (Salt Lake City: Bookcraft, 1960).

# Chapter III:
Unitarian Universalism

Author: Alan W. Gomes; summary by Alan W. Gomes

Background

The Unitarian Universalist Association (UUA) is an association of fellowships, churches, and societies that subscribe to certain broad principles and affiliate themselves organizationally with the UUA denomination, headquartered in Boston, Massachusetts. They are called "Unitarians" because of their historic denial of the Trinity and "Universalists" because of their belief in the ultimate, universal salvation of all humanity. Tracing their roots back to the sixteenth-century Reformation, the Unitarian movement spread from Continental Europe to England and then to America.

Today's UUA is pluralistic, meaning that the group tolerates a wide diversity of beliefs. The UUA comprises theists, Neo-pagans, liberal "Christians," religious humanists, atheists, and more. Officially, there are about 212,000 Unitarian Universalists (UUs), though surveys indicate twice as many professing UUs (that is, one in two UUs is not an "official" member). UUs are at or near the top of religious groups in most social measures (such as median family income, college education, home ownership). Active politically, they champion liberal social causes such as gay and abortion rights, doctor-assisted suicide, and radical feminism. After years of declining or stagnant membership, the UUA is now growing significantly and is making concerted, aggressive, and unprecedented efforts at proselytizing and outreach.

Summary of Beliefs

(UU belief is difficult to classify because a wide range of opinion is found. Because the UUA is pluralistic, there is no one "official" UU position on any particular doctrine. What follows are some of the more common views found in the UUA today.)

Concerning **religious freedom and tolerance,** UUs believe that people should be free both to choose and to craft their own religious beliefs. UUs eschew religious exclusivism. Consequently, UUs reject **the Bible and Christianity** as exclusively true (if true at all). Some (though not all) UUs find inspiring "truths" in the Bible (interpreted through their liberal lens). The Bible is but one of many sacred books that may reveal divine truth, though it is a human book with many errors. All religious truth claims, from whatever source, must be tested by reason, conscience, and personal experience; all doctrines that do not conform to these must be rejected.

Concerning **God,** some Unitarian Universalists are atheists. Others define God (in whole or in part) as a higher power or "divine spark" within them. Some believe that "God" is the term for an ordering principle in nature. A Neopagan view of God (or the Goddess) is an increasingly popular option for many UUs. Whatever their belief about God, UUs are unanimous in their rejection of the orthodox doctrine of the Trinity. **Jesus Christ** was not divine in any special sense; others can, did, and will attain to his spiritual stature. UUs reject Christ's miracles, virgin birth, and bodily resurrection. Like all human teachers, Jesus was fallible and should not be taken as the final authority. Many UUs regard Jesus Christ as one of the world's great ethical teachers, though some UUs dispute even this.

Concerning **man and sin,** UUs affirm the dignity and worth of all human beings. UUs also teach that human beings are the products of evolution. They deny original sin and emphasize human ability to do good. UUs reject **"salvation"** in the biblical sense. All people are God's children. It is arrogant and narrow-minded to say that Jesus is the only way of salvation. "Salvation" consists in making this present world a better place. Human beings can "save" themselves through their own moral character. Many if not most UUs reject the existence of an **afterlife,** focusing their attention on this present life rather than on a hypothetical life in an age to come. They deny the bodily **resurrection** and **hell.** There is no future judgment; people are compensated in this life for what they do.

Parallel Comparison Chart

Unitarian Universalism	The Bible

Divine Revelation and the Bible

Unitarian Universalism	The Bible
"THE TRUTH is not accessible to human grasp" (Owen-Towle).	"Jesus answered, 'I am the way and the truth and the life. No one comes to the Father except through me'" (John 14:6).
"We believe that personal experience, conscience and reason should be the final authorities in religion" (*We Are Unitarian Universalists*).	"Trust in the LORD with all your heart and lean not on your own understanding" (Prov. 3:5).
"We carry our own light with us, and so we are never at a loss for our directions.... We do not rely upon external light" (Marshall, *Challenge*, 45).	"Your word is a lamp to my feet and a light for my path" (Ps. 119:105).
	"Their minds and consciences are corrupted" (Titus 1:15).

"No one of the four Christs of the four gospels is the real Jesus through and through. Those Christs are theological concoctions made up in some part out of historical scraps of information about Jesus but in a greater part out of Christian faith and the polemical, apologetic, and idiosyncratic interests of each gospel writer. The frustrating, deplorable result of this, plus the everlasting paucity of the historical record, is that the real Jesus can never stand up to our inspection and questioning" (McKown, 62–63).

"The Bible is, in its core and essence, a myth" (Straube, 23).

"... they [the biblical writers] used symbolic language, or 'mythology'" (Schulman).

"Therefore, since I myself have carefully investigated everything from the beginning, it seemed good also to me to write an orderly account for you, most excellent Theophilus, so that you may know the certainty of the things you have been taught" (Luke 1:3–4).

"We are witnesses of everything he did in the country of the Jews and in Jerusalem" (Acts 10:39).

"We did not follow cleverly invented stories [Greek *muthois*] when we told you about the power and coming of our Lord Jesus Christ, but we were eyewitnesses of his majesty" (2 Peter 1:16).

(See also 2 Timothy 4:4.)

The Christian Faith

"It takes courage not to settle for a religion 'once for all delivered to the saints'" (Marshall, *Challenge*, 18).

"The following of almost any religion can help a dedicated individual find a better and more meaningful life" (Chworowsky and Raible, 272).

"One thing, however, there is not: an ideology, a theological/religious faith stance, which our congregations have in common" (Hoehler, 6–7).

"Earnestly contend for the faith which was once delivered unto the saints" (Jude 3).

"There is a way that seems right to a man, but in the end it leads to death" (Prov. 14:12; 16:25).

"Enter through the narrow gate. For wide is the gate and broad is the road that leads to destruction, and many enter through it" (Matt. 7:13).

"Do two walk together unless they have agreed to do so?" (Amos 3:3).

"Do not be yoked together with unbelievers" (2 Cor. 6:14).

(See also 1 Corinthians 1:10.)

21

God

"People call God by many names. I call God, Jesus. I accept that you may have another name for god. Jesus is God to me" (Ellis-Hagler, 7).

"In their [i.e., UU] churches are agnostics, humanists, even atheists—as well as nature worshippers, pantheists, and those who affirm a personal God" (Chworowsky and Raible, 265).

". . . many Unitarian Universalists simply do not find a concept of God helpful to religious life" (Beattie, 9–10).

"Most of us do not believe in a supernatural, supreme being who can directly intervene in and alter human life or the mechanism of the natural world" (Sias, 2–3).

"In general, Unitarian Universalists . . . think of God as a unity rather than a trinity" (Chworowsky and Raible, 263–64).

"Paul was decidedly no trinitarian in the accepted traditional sense of the word. Special, Jesus was, but he was not God" (Trudinger, 57).

"Then you call on the name of your god, and I will call on the name of the LORD" (1 Kings 18:24).

". . . his name is the LORD—and rejoice before him" (Ps. 68:4).

"The fool says in his heart, 'There is no God'" (Ps. 14:1).

"They exchanged the truth of God for a lie, and worshiped and served created things rather than the Creator—who is forever praised. Amen. Because of this, God gave them over to shameful lusts" (Rom. 1:25–26).

"Then the LORD rained down burning sulfur on Sodom and Gomorrah—from the LORD out of the heavens" (Gen. 19:24).

"For he received honor and glory from God the Father" (2 Peter 1:17).

"Christ, who is God over all" (Rom. 9:5); "the Word was God" (John 1:1).

". . . you have lied to the Holy Spirit. . . . You have not lied to men but to God" (Acts 5:3–4).

". . . we wait for the blessed hope—the glorious appearing of our great God and Savior, Jesus Christ" (Titus 2:13).

"For in Christ all the fullness of the Deity lives in bodily form" (Col. 2:9).

Jesus Christ

". . . the world has many saviors" (Larsen, "Evangelizing Our Children," 128).

"Jesus answered, 'I am the way and the truth and the life. No one comes to the Father except through me'" (John 14:6).

"Salvation is found in no one else, for there is no other name under heaven

"[Jesus was] a very special man, chosen to be indwelt by 'the Christ'" (Trudinger, 57).

"We do not believe that Jesus Christ was born of a virgin, performed miracles and was resurrected from death" (Sias, 3–4).

"In general, Unitarian Universalists ... honor the ethical leadership of Jesus without considering him to be their final religious authority" (Chworowsky and Raible, 263–64).

given to men by which we must be saved" (Acts 4:12).

"'You *are* the Christ, the Son of the living God'" (Matt. 16:16).

"... he *is* Christ the Lord" (Luke 2:11).

"The virgin will be with child and will give birth to a son, and will call him Immanuel" (Isa. 7:14; cf. Matt. 1:23).

"The miracles I do in my Father's name speak for me" (John 10:25).

"He is not here; he has risen, just as he said" (Matt. 28:6).

"There is a judge for the one who rejects me and does not accept my words; that very word which I spoke will condemn him at the last day" (John 12:48.)

(See also John 5:27; Acts 10:42; 17:31; 2 Timothy 4:1.)

Man and Sin

"Come return to your place in the pews, and hear our heretical views: You were not born in sin so lift up your chin, you have only your dogmas to lose" (Sias, 1).

"Unitarian Universalists reject the traditional Christian idea that the original sin of disobedience of Adam is inherited by all" (Chworowsky and Raible, 2673–68).

"Potentially, the Divine Spirit is present in all human beings" (Higgins et al.).

"Many believe in a spirit of life or a power within themselves, which some choose to call God" (Sias, 2–3).

"Surely I was sinful at birth, sinful from the time my mother conceived me" (Ps. 51:5).

"For just as through the disobedience of the one man the many were made sinners, so also through the obedience of the one man the many will be made righteous" (Rom. 5:19).

"This is what the Sovereign LORD says: 'In the pride of your heart you say, "I am a god; I sit on the throne of a god in the heart of the seas."' But you are a man and not a god, though you think you are as wise as a god.... You will be but a man, not a god, in the hands of those who slay you" (Ezek. 28:2, 9b).

23

Man and Sin (cont.)

"To be perfect is impossible. God forgives our imperfections because we were created that way. It's all right to be human" (Buehrens, 134).

"I said, 'You are "gods"; you are all sons of the Most High.' But you will die like mere men" (Ps. 82:6–7).

"This only have I found: God made mankind upright, but men have gone in search of many schemes" (Eccl. 7:29).

Salvation

"Rather than feel bound by human weaknesses and frailties, we emphasize human strengths.... You might call it a 'can do' religion" (Sias, 13).

"Unitarian Universalism believes in 'salvation by character'" (Marshall, *Challenge*, 31).

"... our moral fiber is equal to all demands" (ibid., 47).

"It [Unitarianism] sees each as the child of God or, as many of us would say, as the child of the universe" (ibid., 31).

Robert Fulghum, Unitarian minister and best-selling author, states, "We're all sons of God" (Religious News Service).

"Unitarian Universalists reject the idea that God sacrificed Jesus 'His Son' to 'atone' for human 'sin'" (Chworowsky and Raible, 267–68).

"... you were dead in your transgressions and sins" (Eph. 2:1).

"apart from me you can do nothing" (John 15:5b).

"If you, O LORD, kept a record of sins, O Lord, who could stand?" (Ps. 130:3).

"For it is by grace you have been saved, through faith—and this not from yourselves, it is the gift of God—not by works, so that no one can boast" (Eph. 2:8–9).

"For all have sinned and fall short of the glory of God" (Rom. 3:23).

"... to those who believed in his name, he gave the right to become children of God" (John 1:12).

"You [unbelieving Pharisees] belong to your father, the devil" (John 8:44).

"Without the shedding of blood there is no forgiveness" (Heb. 9:22).

"The belief that Jesus atoned for the sins of the world by his death has little relevance for us" (Sias, 21).

"Jesus did not think of himself as a Savior offering a blood atonement" (Marshall, *Challenge*, 229).

"Whom God hath set forth to be a propitiation through faith in his blood" (Rom. 3:25 KJV).

"In him we have redemption through his blood, the forgiveness of sins" (Eph. 1:7).

"The blood of Jesus, his Son, purifies us from every sin" (1 John 1:7).

(See also Revelation 1:5; 5:9.)

Heaven, Hell, and the Afterlife

"We simply do not know.... it is common to hear said, 'No one has ever returned to tell us about the afterlife'" (Marshall, "Unitarian Universalism," 300).

"There is enough hell in this world without creating an imaginary hell in another world" (Marshall, "Unitarian Universalism," 231).

"[Unitarian Universalists] are concerned about this life, not an afterlife.... this natural world is the center of our lives" (ibid., 237).

"We do not accept the idea of a physical resurrection" (Sias, 21).

"After his suffering, he showed himself to these men and gave many convincing proofs that he was alive" (Acts 1:3).

"God has raised this Jesus to life, and we are all witnesses of the fact" (Acts 2:32).

"Then he will say to those on his left, 'Depart from me, you who are cursed, into the eternal fire prepared for the devil and his angels'" (Matt. 25:41).

"And the smoke of their torment rises for ever and ever" (Rev. 14:11).

"But seek first his kingdom and his righteousness, and all these things will be given to you as well" (Matt. 6:33).

"Do not store up for yourselves treasures on earth.... But store up for yourselves treasures in heaven" (Matt. 6:19–20a).

"Jesus answered them, 'Destroy this temple, and I will raise it again in three days....' But the temple he had spoken of was his body" (John 2:19, 21).

"Look at my hands and my feet. It is I myself! Touch me and see; a ghost does not have flesh and bones, as you see I have" (Luke 24:39).

Heaven, Hell, and the Afterlife (cont.)

"What happens at the end of time and/or at a Judgment Day? . . . No one knows, but a loving God would not condemn any person to eternal damnation" (Johnson and McGee, 335, 338).

"If you hear someone preaching hellfire and damnation. . . . chances are it's not a Unitarian Universalist!" (Schulz, 3).

"When it comes to a god who would condemn souls to hell, I'm an atheist. I can't believe in that kind of deity" (Larsen, *A Catechism*, 5).

"We believe that human beings should be accountable for their actions and make amends for any harm they may bring to others. But we don't believe that God will punish them" (Sias, 13).

"No one 'goes' to hell; people create their own hells here on earth" (Johnson and McGee, 333, 335).

"Reward and punishment are in this life, in the here and now" (Marshall, "Unitarian Universalist," 300).

"And after my skin has been destroyed, yet in my flesh I will see God; I myself will see him with my own eyes—I, and not another" (Job 19:26–27).

"But the cowardly, the unbelieving, the vile, the murderers, the sexually immoral, those who practice magic arts, the idolaters and all liars—their place will be in the fiery lake of burning sulfur" (Rev. 21:8).

"Then he will say to those on his left, 'Depart from me, you who are cursed, into the eternal fire prepared for the devil and his angels'" (Matt. 25:41).

"And the smoke of their torment rises for ever and ever" (Rev. 14:11).

"[God] will punish those who do not know God and do not obey the gospel of our Lord Jesus. They will be punished with everlasting destruction and shut out from the presence of the Lord and from the majesty of his power" (2 Thess. 1:7–9).

"Just as man is destined to die once, and after that to face judgment" (Heb. 9:27).

"If anyone's name was not found written in the book of life, he was thrown into the lake of fire" (Rev. 20:15).

Sources

Paul H. Beattie, "Personal Choice," in *Unitarian Universalist Views of God,* ed. Doris Hunter (Boston: Unitarian Universalist Association, n.d.).

Karl M. Chworowsky and Christopher Gist Raible, "What Is a Unitarian Universalist?" in *Religions in America,* ed. Leo Rosten (New York: Simon and Schuster, 1975).

Elizabeth Ellis-Hagler, "George Met Jesus in the Charles Street Jail: The Bible in Human Transformation," *The Unitarian Universalist Christian* 44, no. 1 (Spring 1989).

Daniel G. Higgins Jr. et al., *Unitarian Universalist Views of Jesus* (Boston: Unitarian Universalist Association, 1994).

Harry H. Hoehler, "Is There a Place for UU Christians in the UUA? A Reply and Some Reflections," *Unitarian Universalist Christian* 38, nos. 3–4 (Fall-Winter 1983).

Christopher Jay Johnson and Marsha G. McGee, eds., *Encounters with Eternity: Religious Views of Death and Life After-Death* (New York: Philosophical Library, 1986).

Tony Larsen, "Evangelizing Our Children," in *Salted with Fire: Unitarian Universalist Strategies for Sharing Faith and Growing Congregations,* ed. Scott W. Alexander (Boston: Skinner House, 1995).

Tony Larsen with Ellen Schmidt, *A Catechism for Unitarian Universalists (Leader Guide)* (Boston: Unitarian Universalist Association, 1989).

Marjorie Newlin Leaming, quoted in John A. Buehrens, "Expectations," in *Our Chosen Faith: An Introduction to Unitarian Universalism,* eds. John A. Buehrens and F. Forrester Church (Boston: Beacon, 1989).

Delos B. McKown, "A Humanist Looks at the future of Unitarian Universalism," *Religious Humanism* 20, no. 2 (Spring 1986).

George N. Marshall, *Challenge of a Liberal Faith,* rev. and enl. ed. (New Canaan, Conn.: Keats Publishing, 1980).

George N. Marshall, "Unitarian Universalism," in *Encounters with Eternity: Religious Views of Death and Life After-Death,* eds. Christopher Jay Johnson and Marsha G. McGee (New York: Philosophical Library, 1986).

Tom Owen-Towle, *Welcome to Unitarian Universalism: A Community of Truth, Service, Holiness and Love* (Boston: Unitarian Universalist Association, n.d.).

Religious News Service, "'Kindergarten' Writer Says Point Was Missed," *Los Angeles Times,* 21 December 1991, Orange County Edition, Special section, S-7.

J. Frank Schulman, "An Affirmation that Life has Meaning," in *Unitarian Universalist Views of the Bible,* ed. Daniel G. Higgins, Jr. (Boston: Unitarian Universalist Association, 1994).

William F. Schulz, "Our Faith," in *The Unitarian Universalist Pocket Guide,* ed. William F. Schulz, 2d ed. (Boston: Skinner House, 1993).

John Sias from interviews with Rev. Steve Edington, *100 Questions that Non-Members Ask about Unitarian Universalism* (n.p.: Transition Publishing, 1994).

Arvid Straube, "The Bible in Unitarian Universalist Theology," *Unitarian Universalist Christian* 44, no. 1 (1989).

Paul Trudinger, "St. Paul: A Unitarian Universalist Christian?" *Faith and Freedom* 43 (Spring-Summer 1990).

We Are Unitarian Universalists (Boston: Unitarian Universalist Association, 1992).

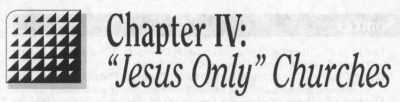

Chapter IV:
"Jesus Only" Churches

Author: E. Calvin Beisner; summary by Alan W. Gomes

Background

"Jesus only" churches are so called because they reject the triune baptismal formula (that is, in the name of the Father, Son, and Holy Spirit), baptizing instead only in Jesus' name. They are also called "Oneness" churches because they believe not only that the Father, Son, and Holy Spirit are one in substance (as Trinitarians believe) but also that they are one in person (which Trinitarians reject). Thus, Jesus is the Father, Jesus is the Spirit, the Spirit is the Father, etc. This teaching is also known as "modalism" because the one God (who is also one person) manifests himself successively in three different "modes."

The churches considered here came out of the Assemblies of God (AG) in the second decade of the 1900s. In 1916 the AG adopted a doctrinal statement that clearly stipulated trinitarian belief, thus forcing out Oneness adherents, who then formed their own denominations and associations. Although there are about ninety different Oneness denominations, the United Pentecostal Church International (UPCI) is by far the largest, with just over one million members worldwide.

Summary of Belief

(Because the UPCI is the most prominent Oneness group and has the most developed theological system, the doctrinal critique presented in Professor Beisner's book responds to views expressed by prominent UPCI theologians.)

Concerning **Christ,** Oneness adherents believe that Jesus is fully God; they prove this with many of the same biblical texts that Trinitarians cite. However, unlike Trinitarians, Oneness believers claim that Jesus is the Father and the Holy Spirit, arguing that in the incarnation "all of God" became incarnate. As noted, this is a reintroduction of the ancient heresy known as modalism. As to **Jesus' Sonship,** they maintain that Jesus is the Son (in any sense of the term— either "Son of Man" or "Son of God") only in his incarnation. According to them, the term "Son" refers strictly to Christ's human nature. Thus, Oneness believers deny Christ's eternal, preexistent Sonship. Before the incarnation, God could be designated as the "Word"—who is also the Father—but not as Son. At the incarnation, God assumed the role of Son for the purpose of redemption, but this role will have a definite end (that is, at the end of the age).

Oneness theology denies as illogical and unscriptural the **personal distinctions in the Godhead.** Jesus, the Father, and the Holy Spirit are all one and the same person. Bible verses that appear to reveal distinctions between Jesus and the Father or the Holy Spirit actually reveal distinctions between the divine and human natures of the incarnate Jesus. Concerning **salvation,** Oneness writers agree with historic orthodoxy in affirming that one must be "born again" in order to be saved. However, contrary to the biblical teaching of justification by faith alone, Oneness theology asserts that the new birth takes place through faith, repentance, water baptism, and baptism in the Holy Spirit. **Water baptism,** which is indispensable to salvation, must be by immersion and administered in the name of Jesus only. Likewise, **baptism in the Holy Spirit** is essential to salvation and never occurs without the "initial evidence" of speaking in tongues.

Parallel Comparison Chart

"Jesus Only" Churches	The Bible

Jesus Christ

"... the [title] Son always refers to the Incarnation and we cannot use it in the absence of the human element" (Bernard, *Oneness of God*, 103). "... we can only use the term 'Son of God' correctly when it includes the humanity of Jesus" (Bernard, *Oneness of God*, 99).	"In the past God spoke to our forefathers through the prophets at many times and in various ways, but in these last days he has spoken to us by his Son, ... through whom he made the universe" (Heb. 1:1–2).
"The Sonship began at Bethlehem. The Incarnation was the time when the Sonship began.... Here [in Luke 1:35] it is clearly revealed that the humanity of the Lord Jesus is the Son" (Magee, *Is Jesus*, 32).	"... the Father ... brought us into the kingdom of the Son he loves.... He [the Son] is the image of the invisible God, the firstborn over all creation. For by him [the Son] all things were created ..." (Col. 1:12–16).
"We cannot say that God died, so we cannot say 'God the Son' died. On the other hand, we can say that the Son of God died because Son refers to humanity" (Bernard, *Oneness of God*, 100).	"Be shepherds of the church of God, which he bought with his own blood" (Acts 20:28). "'I am the Alpha and the Omega,' says the Lord God, 'who is, and who was, and who is to come, the Almighty'" (Rev. 1:8). "I am the First and the Last. I am the Living One; I was dead, and behold I am alive for ever and ever!" (Rev. 1:17–18). "These are the words of him

29

Jesus Christ (cont.)

who is the First and the Last, who died and came to life again" (Rev. 2:8). "[Jesus said,] 'I am the Alpha and the Omega, the First and the Last, the Beginning and the End'" (Rev. 22:13).

The Trinity

"... Jesus Himself taught that He was the Father" (Bernard, *Oneness of God*, 67).

"If there is only one God and that God is the Father (Malachi 2:10), and if Jesus is God, then it logically follows that Jesus is the Father" (Bernard, *Oneness of God*, 66).

"The Holy Spirit is the Spirit that was incarnated in Jesus and is Jesus in Spirit form ..." (Bernard, *Oneness and Trinity*, 10).

"If I testify about myself, my testimony is not valid. There is another who testifies in my favor, and I know that his testimony about me is valid.... And the Father who sent me has himself testified concerning me" (John 5:31–32, 37).

"In your own Law it is written that the testimony of two men is valid. I am one who testifies for myself; my other witness is the Father, who sent me" (John 8:17–18).

"Father, the time has come. Glorify your Son, that your Son may glorify you.... And now, Father, glorify me in your presence with the glory I had with you before the world began" (John 17:1, 5).

"... I will ask the Father, and he will give you *another* Counselor to be with you forever—the Spirit of truth" (John 14:16–17).

"When the Counselor comes, whom *I* will send to you from the Father, the Spirit of truth who goes out from the Father, *he* will testify about *me*" (John 15:26).

"But when he, the Spirit of truth, comes, he will guide you into all truth. He will not speak on his own; he will speak only what he hears, and he will tell you what is yet to come. He will bring glory to me by taking from what is mine and making it known to you. All

"The oneness of God is not a mystery.... The triune nature of God is an incomprehensible mystery" (Bernard, *Oneness and Trinity*, 14).

that belongs to the Father is mine. That is why I said the Spirit will take from what is mine and make it known to you" (John 16:13–15).

"Beyond all question, the mystery of godliness is great: He appeared in a body, was vindicated by the Spirit, was seen by angels, was preached among the nations, was believed on in the world, was taken up in glory" (1 Tim. 3:16; see 1 Cor. 4:1; Col. 2:2).

"In the beginning was the Word, and the Word was with God, and the Word was God.... In him was life, and that life was the light of men. The light shines in the darkness, but the darkness has not understood it.... The true light that gives light to every man was coming into the world. He was in the world, and though the world was made through him, the world did not recognize him....

"No one has ever seen God, but God the One and Only, who is at the Father's side, has made him known" (John 1:1, 4–5, 9–10, 18).*

Salvation

"Water baptism is a part of that process by which a man is born into, or made a part of, the kingdom of God" (Clanton et al., *Bible Doctrines*, 79).

"But when the kindness and love of God our Savior appeared, he saved us, not because of righteous things we had done, but because of his mercy. He saved us through the washing of rebirth and renewal by the Holy Spirit, whom he poured out on us generously through Jesus Christ our Savior, so that, having been justified by his grace, we might become heirs having the hope of eternal life" (Titus 3:4–7).

---

*The Greek word *mustērion* may denote something too profound to be understood by human reason, or something once hidden but then revealed by God (Bauer, *Lexicon*, 530–31). That the doctrine of the Trinity is a mystery is entirely consistent with what Scripture reveals about the incomprehensible, yet revealed, mystery of God's becoming man in Christ.

Salvation (cont.)

"I am thankful that I did not baptize any of you except Crispus and Gaius, so no one can say that you were baptized into my name.... For Christ did not send me to baptize, but to preach the gospel ..." (1 Cor. 1:14–15, 17).

"... we are baptized in order to obtain the remission of our sins" (Williams, *Bible Plan*, 11).

"... a man is justified by faith apart from observing the law" (Rom. 3:28).

"There are several things man must do in order to be saved. He must hear the gospel preached, he must repent, he must believe, he must obey God's Word, and *he must be baptized in Jesus name* [emphasis added]" (Clanton et al., *Salvation*, 119.)

"Is this blessedness only for the circumcised, or also for the uncircumcised? We have been saying that Abraham's faith was credited to him as righteousness. Under what circumstances was it credited? Was it after he was circumcised, or before? It was not after, but before! And he received the sign of circumcision, a seal of the righteousness that he had by faith while he was still uncircumcised" (Rom. 4:9–11).

"Baptism is *part of our spiritual circumcision* [emphasis original], or initiation into the new covenant (Colossians 2:11-13). Under the old covenant a male child officially received his name at his physical circumcision. (See Luke 2:21.) Water baptism is the time when our new family name is invoked upon us at our spiritual circumcision" (Bernard, *In the Name of Jesus*, 51).

"Water baptism is correctly administered by saying 'in the name of Jesus'" (Bernard, *Oneness of God*, 295).

"Therefore go and make disciples of all nations, baptizing them in the name of the Father and of the Son and of the Holy Spirit, and teaching them to obey everything I have commanded you" (Matt. 28:19–20).

"In later centuries, when attempts were made to teach a 'trinity' of persons in the Godhead, the baptismal formula was adapted to emphasize the three persons in a supposed 'trinity'" (Clanton et al., *Bible Doctrines*, 84).

"The baptism with, by, in, or of the Holy Ghost (Holy Spirit) is part of New Testament salvation, not an optional, postconversional experience (John 3:5; Romans 8:1–16; Ephesians 1:13–14; Titus 3:5)" (Bernard, *Essentials*, 19).

"Again Jesus said, 'Peace be with you! As the Father has sent me, I am sending you.' And with that he breathed on them [the disciples] and said, 'Receive the Holy Spirit'" (John 20:21–22).

"On one occasion, while he was eating with them, he [said to them]: '... in a few days you will be baptized with the Holy Spirit.... But you will receive power when the Holy Spirit comes on you...'" (Acts 1:4–5, 8).

"You, however, are controlled not by the sinful nature but by the Spirit, if the Spirit of God lives in you.... And if the Spirit of him who raised Jesus from the dead is living in you, he who raised Christ from the dead will also give life to your mortal bodies through his Spirit, who lives in you" (Rom. 8:9, 11).

"And you also were included in Christ when you heard the word of truth, the gospel of your salvation. Having believed, you were marked in him with a seal, the promised Holy Spirit, who is a deposit guaranteeing our inheritance ..." (Eph. 1:13–14).

"Anyone who has never spoken in tongues has never been baptized with the Holy Ghost" (Reynolds, *Truth*, 53–4). (And if baptism with the Holy Spirit is "part of New Testament salvation" [Bernard, *Essentials*, 19], then whoever has not spoken in tongues is not saved.)

"Everyone who calls on the name of the Lord will be saved" (Rom. 10:13).

"Paul, ... to the church of God which is at Corinth, to those who have been sanctified in Christ Jesus, saints by calling, with all who in every place call upon the name of our Lord Jesus Christ... Now you are Christ's body, and individually members of it. And God has appointed in the church, first apostles, second prophets, third teachers, then miracles, then gifts of healings, helps, administrations, various kinds of tongues. All are not apostles, are they?... All do not speak with tongues, do they?" (1 Cor. 1:1–2; 12:27–30, NASB).

33

Sources

Walter Bauer, *A Greek-English Lexicon of the New Testament and Other Early Christian Literature,* 2d ed., trans. W. F. Arndt and F. W. Gingrich, rev. F. W. Gingrich and F. W. Danker (1957; reprint, Chicago: University of Chicago Press, 1979).

David K. Bernard, *Essentials of the New Birth* (Hazelwood, Mo.: Word Aflame Press, 1987).

David K. Bernard, *In the Name of Jesus* (Hazelwood, Mo.: Word Aflame Press, 1992).

David K. Bernard, *Oneness and Trinity* A.D. *100–300: The Doctrine of God in Ancient Christian Writings* (Hazelwood, Mo.: Word Aflame Press, 19917).

David K. Bernard, *The Oneness of God* (Hazelwood, Mo.: Word Aflame Press, 1983).

Charles Clanton, Crawford Coon, and Paul Dugas, *Bible Doctrines: Foundation of the Church* (Hazelwood, Mo.: Word Aflame Press, 1984).

Charles Clanton, Dennis Croucher, and Paul Dugas, *Salvation: Key to Eternal Life* (Hazelwood, Mo.: Word Aflame Press, 1985).

Gordon Magee, *Is Jesus in the Godhead or is the Godhead in Jesus?* (Hazelwood, Mo.: Word Aflame Press, 1988).

Carl E. Williams, *The Bible Plan of Salvation* (Hazelwood, Mo.: Word Aflame Press, 1988).

Ralph Vincent Reynolds, *Truth Shall Triumph: A Study of Pentecostal Doctrines* (Hazelwood, Mo.: Word Aflame Press, 1965).

 # Chapter V:
Unification Church

Author: J. Isamu Yamamoto; summary by Alan W. Gomes

Background

The founder and current leader of the Unification Church is Sun Myung Moon. Moon claims that in 1936, when he was sixteen, Jesus Christ appeared to him and declared that Moon would complete the mission Jesus had only begun. In 1946 Moon was arrested by the North Korean police and, Moon claims, tortured for his faith. Released and then sentenced again to prison, he managed to escape to the south during the Korean War. He founded his church in South Korea in 1954, which he named the Holy Spirit Association for the Unification of World Christianity (most commonly known as simply the Unification Church). In 1957, Moon published the *Divine Principle,* which is the main authoritative work setting forth Unification (i.e., Moon's) theology.

In 1959 the group spread to the United States. Moon drew his biggest following in America in the 1970s, where his movement garnered considerable media attention, much of it negative. Controversies swirled around alleged unethical recruitment and fund-raising tactics and Moon's authoritarian leadership style. In 1982 Moon began serving eighteen months in federal prison on tax-evasion charges.

The Unification Church has somewhere between one and two million members, of whom ten to thirty thousand reside in the United States. By far the largest concentration of "Moonies," as they are commonly called by outsiders, is in Korea and Japan. The church runs the Unification Theological Seminary in New York and has considerable business holdings, including the well-known daily newspaper the *Washington Times.*

Summary of Beliefs

Concerning **divine revelation,** the Unification Church teaches that God has revealed his truth to Moon, God's source of spiritual truth for this present age. Moon's truth is especially found in the *Divine Principle,* which is the "third testament" of the Bible; it is as—indeed more—authoritative than the Bible. Concerning **sin,** Moon teaches that God's original plan was for Adam and Eve to mature spiritually and then to procreate a sinless human race. However, Satan thwarted this plan by seducing Eve to have illicit sexual intercourse with him; this led to the spiritual corruption of mankind. Then, when Adam in turn had sex with Eve (before reaching spiritual maturity), this led to mankind's physical corruption.

Salvation therefore requires both spiritual and physical redemption. Jesus Christ came to earth to accomplish both elements: He was to marry and produce a sinless race, which would be redeemed both physically and spiritually. However, because he ran afoul of his Jewish contemporaries, Jesus could not accomplish man's total salvation and so opted to secure only spiritual salvation by dying on the cross. It therefore remains for a second messiah, the "Lord of the Second Advent," to provide physical salvation. Most Unification Church members identify Moon as the Lord of the Second Advent. Moon's mission is to produce a perfect family (indeed, his twelve children are considered sinless) and to extend this perfection to his followers through their obedience to him (such as having their marriages arranged and blessed by Moon).

Concerning **Jesus Christ,** Moon denies that Jesus is truly God or equal to the Father, though he did attain perfection and is in that sense "divine." The biblical doctrine of the **Trinity** is denied. Christ's **resurrection** was not physical, nor does it accomplish our physical redemption. Christ was raised as a spirit, and his resurrection accomplishes the redemption of our spirits. Regarding the **afterlife,** Moon teaches that hell is ruled by Satan and is the place where the spirits of the dead who have rejected God dwell. Since the Lord of the Second Advent will eventually redeem all mankind, hell will be abolished. Ultimately, all human beings will become divine spirits and dwell in heaven with God.

Parallel Comparison Chart

Unification Church	The Bible
### Divine Revelation	
"With the fullness of time, God has sent His messenger to resolve the fundamental questions of life and the universe. His name is Sun Myung Moon. . . . We have recorded here [in the *Divine Principle*] what Sun Myung Moon's disciples have hitherto heard and witnessed" (*Divine Principle*, 16).	"See to it that no one takes you captive through hollow and deceptive philosophy, which depends on human tradition and the basic principles of this world rather than on Christ" (Col. 2:8).
"God revealed to Reverend Moon the fundamental core of his teaching" (Young Oon Kim, *Unification Theology*, 50).	"If anyone teaches false doctrines and does not agree to the sound instruction of our Lord Jesus Christ and to godly teaching, he is conceited and understands nothing" (1 Tim. 6:3–4).
"It may be displeasing to religious believers, especially to Christians, to learn	"All Scripture is God-breathed" (2 Tim. 3:16).

that a new expression of truth must appear. They believe that the Bible, which they now have, is perfect and absolute in itself. Truth, of course, is unique, eternal, unchangeable, and absolute. The Bible, however, is not the truth itself, but a textbook teaching the truth" (*Divine Principle*, 9).

"Your word is truth" (John 17:17).

"Christians of today, who are captives to scriptural words, will surely criticize the words and conduct of the Lord of the Second Advent [Sun Myung Moon], according to the limits of what the New Testament words literally state.... Innumerable Christians of today are dashing on the way which they think will lead them to the Kingdom of Heaven. Nevertheless, this very road is apt to lead them to Hell" (*Divine Principle*, 533, 535).

"Dear friends, do not believe every spirit, but test the spirits to see whether they are from God, because many false prophets have gone out into the world" (1 John 4:1).

Sin

"Many Christians to this day believe that the fruit which caused Adam and Eve to fall was literally the fruit of a tree.... According to what has been elucidated by the Bible, we have come to understand that the root of sin is not that the first human ancestors ate a fruit, but that they had an illicit blood relationship with an angel symbolized by a serpent" (*Divine Principle*, 66, 75).

"When the woman saw that the fruit of the tree was good for food and pleasing to the eye, and also desirable for gaining wisdom, she took some and ate it. She also gave some to her husband, who was with her, and he ate it" (Gen. 3:6).

"The root of man's sin stems from adultery.... Every religion which teaches how to eliminate sin has called adultery the greatest sin.... This also demonstrates that the root of sin lies in adultery" (*Divine Principle*, 75).

"For whoever keeps the whole law and yet stumbles at just one point is guilty of breaking all of it. For he who said, 'Do not commit adultery,' also said, 'Do not murder.' If you do not commit adultery but do commit murder, you have become a lawbreaker" (James 2:10–11).

"Men, without exception, are inclined to repel evil and to pursue goodness" (*Divine Principle*, 65).

"There is no one righteous, not even one; there is no one who understands, no one who seeks God. All have turned away, they have together become worthless; there is no one who does good, not even one" (Rom. 3:10–12; see also Pss. 14:1–3; 53:1–3; Eccl. 7:20).

37

Sin (cont.)

"Father [Moon] is sinless, Mother [Moon's wife] is sinless, and their children are sinless" (Ken Sudo, "Christology," from *The 120–Day Training Manual*, 236).

"There is no one who does not sin" (1 Kings 8:46).

"If we claim to be without sin, we deceive ourselves and the truth is not in us. . . . If we claim we have not sinned, we make him out to be a liar and his word has no place in our lives" (1 John 1:8, 10).

Salvation

"From the time of Jesus through the present, all Christians have thought that Jesus came to the world to die. This is because they did not know the fundamental purpose of Jesus' coming as the Messiah, and entertained the wrong idea that spiritual salvation was the only mission for which Jesus came to the world. . . . Jesus did not come to die" (*Divine Principle*, 152).

"Jesus was then resolved to take the cross as the condition of indemnity to pay for the accomplishment of even the spiritual salvation of man when he found that he was unable to accomplish the providence of both spiritual and physical salvation" (*Divine Principle*, 151).

"The original self will be restored by removing man's original sin through the Second Advent of the Lord. . . . We know that now is truly the time for Christ to come again" (*Divine Principle*, 180, 498–99).

"Who could be the male child who is born of a woman with the qualification of sitting on the throne of God, and who will rule all the nations with the words of God? This can be none other than the Lord of the Second Advent who is to be

"How foolish you are, and how slow of heart to believe all that the prophets have spoken! Did not the Christ have to suffer these things and then enter his glory?" (Luke 24:25–26).

"This man was handed over to you by God's set purpose and foreknowledge; and you, with the help of wicked men, put him to death by nailing him to the cross" (Acts 2:23).

"The blood of Jesus, his [God's] Son, purifies us from all sin" (1 John 1:7).

"Christ was sacrificed once to take away the sins of many people; and he will appear a second time, not to bear sin, but to bring salvation to those who are waiting for him" (Heb. 9:28).

"It is by the name of Jesus Christ of Nazareth, whom you crucified but whom God raised from the dead, that this man stands before you healed. . . . Salvation is found in no one else, for there is no other name under heaven born on the earth as the King of Kings, and who will realize the Kingdom of God on earth.... [He] must come again in order to complete the physical salvation" (*Divine Principle*, 509, 512).

"Therefore, the Lord of the Second Advent must come to restore the whole of mankind to be children of God's direct lineage" (*Divine Principle*, 369).

"Rev. Moon is the Messiah, the Lord of the Second Advent" (Ken Sudo, "Family Problems," from *The 120–Day Training Manual*, 160).

"We atone for our sins through specific acts of penance" (Young Oon Kim, *Unification Theology*, 230).

"Man's perfection must be accomplished finally by his own effort without God's help" (Kwang-Yol Yoo, *New Hope News* [October 7, 1974], 7).

given to men by which we must be saved" (Acts 4:10, 12).

"Yet to all who received him, to those who believed in his [Jesus'] name, he gave the right to become children of God" (John 1:12).

"Jesus answered, 'I am the way and the truth and the life. No one comes to the Father except through me'" (John 14:6).

"For it is by grace you have been saved, through faith—and this not from yourselves, it is the gift of God—not by works, so that no one can boast" (Eph. 2:8–9).

The Deity of Jesus Christ and the Trinity

"However great [Jesus'] value may be, he cannot assume a value greater than that of a man who has attained the purpose of creation" (*Divine Principle*, 209).

"Jesus, from his outward appearance, was no different from ordinary, fallen men" (*Divine Principle*, 171).

"Jesus, on earth, was a man no different from us except for the fact that he was without original sin. Even in the spirit world after his resurrection, he lives as a spirit man with his disciples.... Jesus is not God Himself" (*Divine Principle*, 212).

"He [Jesus] is the image of the invisible God, the firstborn over all creation. For by him all things were created: things in heaven and on earth, visible and invisible, whether thrones or powers or rulers or authorities; all things were created by him" (Col. 1:15–16).

"For in Christ all the fullness of the Deity lives in bodily form" (Col. 2:9).

"I [Jesus] and the Father are one" (John 10:30).

"To those who through the righteousness of our God and Savior Jesus Christ have received a faith as precious as ours" (2 Peter 1:1).

"In the beginning was the Word, and the Word was with God and the Word [Jesus] was God.... The Word became flesh and made his dwelling among us" (John 1:1, 14).

The Deity of Jesus Christ and the Trinity (cont.)

"Jesus himself says that Heung Jin Nim [Moon's deceased son] is the new Christ [heavenly Messiah]. He is the center of the spirit world now. This means he is in a higher position than Jesus" (Young Whi Kim, *Guidance for Heavenly Tradition* vol. 2, 183).

"Christ [the Lord of the Second Advent] must come again in flesh in order that he may become the True Parent both spiritually and physically, by forming the substantial Trinity centered on God" (*Divine Principle*, 218).

"God exalted him [Jesus] to the highest place and gave him the name that is above every name, that at the name of Jesus every knee should bow, in heaven and on earth and under the earth, and every tongue confess that Jesus Christ is Lord" (Phil. 2:9–11).

"Go and make disciples of all nations, baptizing them in the name of the Father and of the Son and of the Holy Spirit" (Matt. 28:19).

"May the grace of the Lord Jesus Christ, and the love of God, and the fellowship of the Holy Spirit be with you all" (2 Cor. 13:14).

The Resurrection of Jesus Christ

"Because the Jewish people disbelieved Jesus and delivered him up for crucifixion, his body was invaded by Satan, and he was killed. Therefore, even when Christians believe in and become one body with Jesus, whose body was invaded by Satan, their bodies still remain subject to Satan's invasion" (*Divine Principle*, 147–48).

"As we know through the Bible, Jesus after the resurrection was not the same Jesus who had lived with his disciples before his crucifixion. He was no longer a man seen through physical eyes, because he was a being transcendent of time and space" (*Divine Principle*, 360).

"Having disarmed the powers and authorities, he [Jesus] made a public spectacle of them, triumphing over them by the cross" (Col. 2:15).

"They [Jesus' disciples] were startled and frightened, thinking they saw a ghost. He said to them, 'Why are you troubled, and why do doubts rise in your minds? Look at my hands and my feet. It is I myself! Touch me and see; a ghost does not have flesh and bones, as you see I have.' When he had said this, he showed them his hands and feet. And while they still did not believe it because of joy and amazement, he asked them, 'Do you have anything here to eat?' They gave him a piece of broiled fish, and he took it and ate it in their presence" (Luke 24:37–43).

"The physical resurrection and bodily ascension of Jesus ... are not an essential part of ... faith in Jesus as the risen Lord" (Young Oon Kim, *Unification Theology*, 185).

"The Jews demanded of him [Jesus], 'What miraculous sign can you show us to prove your authority to do all this?' Jesus answered them, 'Destroy this temple, and I will raise it again in three days.' The Jews replied, 'It has taken forty-six years to build this temple, and you are going to raise it in three days?' But the temple he had spoken of was his body. After he was raised from the dead, his disciples recalled what he had said. Then they believed the Scripture and the words that Jesus had spoken" (John 2:18–22).

Hell and Heaven

"Hell is a pagan idea totally contrary to the Christian faith in a God of immeasurable love" (Young Oon Kim, *Unification Theology & Christian Thought*, 185).

"Through their works, evil spirit men also are allowed to enter the sphere of benefit of the new age, with the same benefits as earthly men.... The ultimate purpose of God's providence of restoration is to save all mankind. Therefore, it is God's intention to abolish Hell completely" (*Divine Principle*, 187, 190).

"Christians, up to the present, have been confused in their concepts of Heaven and Paradise because they have not known the Principle. If Jesus had accomplished the purpose of his coming on earth as the Messiah, the Kingdom of Heaven on earth would have been established at that time.... The Kingdom of Heaven on earth has not been realized due to the crucifixion of Jesus, and not a single person on earth has attained the divine-spirit stage. Consequently, no spirit man has entered the Heavenly Kingdom of God.... Therefore, the Heavenly Kingdom of God still remains vacant" (*Divine Principle*, 176).

"He [the Lord Jesus] will punish those who do not know God and do not obey the gospel of our Lord Jesus. They will be punished with everlasting destruction and shut out from the presence of the Lord" (2 Thess. 1:8–9).

"Then they [the wicked] will go away to *eternal punishment*, but the righteous to eternal life" (Matt. 25:46, emphasis added).

"Do not let your hearts be troubled. Trust in God; trust also in me. In my Father's house are many rooms; if it were not so, I would have told you. I am going there to prepare a place for you. And if I go and prepare a place for you, I will come back and take you to be with me that you also may be where I am going" (John 14:1–3).

41

Sources

Ken Sudo, "Christology," in *The 120-Day Training Manual* (New York: The Holy Spirit Association for the Unification of World Christianity, n.d.).

Kwang-Yol Yoo, *New Hope News* (October 7, 1974).

Sun Myung Moon, *Divine Principle*, 2d ed. (Washington, D.C.: The Holy Spirit Association for the Unification of World Christianity, 1973).

Young Oon Kim, *Unification Theology* (New York: The Holy Spirit Association for the Unification of World Christianity, 1980).

Young Whi Kim, *Guidance for Heavenly Tradition*, 2 vols. (Mainz, Germany: Vereinigungskirche, 1985).

# Chapter VI:
Masonic Lodge

Authors: George Mather and Larry Nichols;
summary by Alan W. Gomes

Background

The precise origins of the Masonic Lodge (also known as Freemasonry) are difficult to determine. It is likely that the Lodge as it is known today began in early eighteenth-century England. Numerous Lodges sprang up throughout England and in various locations on the Continent. Although the Lodges often cooperated, each was autonomous and governed by its own constitution. The Lodge movement quickly spread to America; several thousand Lodges were formed during the 1800s.

Masons move through different "degrees" of initiation and then become involved in one of two main branches, or "rites." All Masons are initiated into the so-called Blue Lodge, consisting of three degrees. Each of these degrees involves certain prescribed rituals, including the swearing of various oaths; upon successful completion the candidate attains the rank of "Master Mason." Following this, Masons may then pursue additional degrees through either the "York Rite" or the "Scottish Rite," the latter being the more popular. There are also affiliate orders connected with the main body of Freemasonry, such as the Shriners, the Order of the Eastern Star, the Order of DeMolay, and the International Order of Job's Daughters. There are about 2.5 million Master Masons in the United States, roughly 1 million of whom are also in the Scottish Rite. A number of mainline Christian bodies, such Lutherans and Roman Catholics, forbid involvement in the Lodge on the grounds that Lodge teachings are patently unbiblical. Other denominations, such as the Southern Baptists, permit Lodge involvement, in spite of its unbiblical character.

Summary of Beliefs

The older, classic Masonic authors readily granted Freemasonry's **religious status.** However, many modern Masonic writers deny that Masonry is a religion at all. Instead, they argue that Masonry is compatible with a person's chosen faith (whatever that may be) and is even an enhancement to it. These protestations notwithstanding, Freemasonry possesses common and key characteristics of a religion, including prayers, pledges, hymns, readings from sacred literature, a definite view of the afterlife (demonstrated in their own funeral services), teachings on sin and salvation, and more.

Freemasonry is incompatible with biblical Christianity. While Masons claim to revere the **Bible,** they deny that it alone is God's Word. The Bible is a good guide for morality, as are the sacred books of other religions, such as the Koran. **God,** belief in whom is mandatory for Masons, is described variously as the Great Architect of the Universe and the All-Seeing Eye; different religions (including Judaism, Christianity, Islam) all acknowledge this same true deity, even if they address him by different names. **Jesus Christ** is regarded primarily for his ethical teachings. Masons generally do not talk about Christ's deity or the doctrine of the Trinity. Regarding **man and sin,** Masons typically deny the biblical doctrines of original sin and human depravity. They believe that human beings are able to improve their moral character by virtuous living. The practice of Freemasonry provides the means by which this might be accomplished.

Parallel Comparison Chart

Freemasonry	The Bible

The Bible

"The Bible is used among Masons as a symbol of the will of God, however it may be expressed. And, therefore, whatever to any people expresses that will may be used as a substitute for the Bible in a Masonic Lodge. Thus, in a Lodge consisting entirely of Jews, the Old Testament alone may be placed on the altar, and the Turkish Masons make use of the Koran. Whether it be the Gospels to the Christians, the Pentateuch to the Israelites, the Koran to the Muslim, or the Vedas to the Brahman, it everywhere Masonically conveys the same idea—that the symbolism of the Divine will revealed to Man" (Mackey, *Encyclopedia of Freemasonry,* 104).

"The Bible, with all the allegories it contains, expresses, in an incomplete and veiled manner only, the religious science of the Hebrews" (Pike, *Morals and Dogma,* 744).

"Do not add to what I command you and do not subtract from it, but keep the commands of the LORD your God that I give you" (Deut. 4:2).

"I am astonished that you are so quickly deserting the one who called you by the grace of Christ and are turning to a different gospel—which is really no gospel at all. Evidently some people are throwing you into confusion and are trying to pervert the gospel of Christ. But even if we or an angel from heaven should preach a gospel other than the one we preached to you, let him be eternally condemned. As we have already said, so now I say again: If anybody is preaching to you a gospel other than what you accepted, let him be eternally condemned!" (Gal. 1:6–9).

"Your word is a lamp to my feet and a light for my path" (Ps. 119:105).

"But as for you, continue in what you have learned and have become convinced of, because you know those from

"There is no book of which so little is known as the Bible. To most who read it, it is as incomprehensible as the Sohar" (Pike, *Morals and Dogma*, 105).

whom you learned it, and how from infancy you have known the holy Scriptures, which are able to make you wise for salvation through faith in Christ Jesus" (2 Tim. 3:14–15).

"And even if our gospel is veiled, it is veiled to those who are perishing. The god of this age has blinded the minds of unbelievers, so that they cannot see the light of the gospel of the glory of Christ, who is the image of God" (2 Cor. 4:3–4).

God

"Therefore it [Freemasonry] invites to its altar men of all faiths, knowing that, if they use different names for 'the Nameless One of a hundred names,' they are praying to the one God and Father of all" (*Quarterly Bulletin* [July 1915]: 17).

"Masons do not attempt to propagate any creed save their own simple and sublime one of faith in the existence of a Supreme Being and faith in His exalted works; no religion, save the universal, eternal, and immutable religion, such as God planted in the hearts of universal humanity. Masonry's followers are found alike among Christians, Jews, Brahmans, and Turks, for it is in the universal decree that: 'The one Great God looked down and smiled and counted each his loving child. For Turk and Brahman, Monk and Jew, had reached Him thru the God he knew'" (*New Age* [January 1943]: 33).

"This is what the LORD says—Israel's King and Redeemer, the LORD Almighty: I am the first and I am the last; apart from me there is no God" (Isa. 44:6).

"Hear, O Israel: The LORD our God, the LORD is one" (Deut. 6:4).

"I am the LORD your God, who brought you out of Egypt, out of the land of slavery. You shall have no other gods before me" (Ex. 20:2–3).

"Worship the Lord your God, and serve him only" (Matt. 4:10).

"You believe that there is one God. Good! Even the demons believe that—and shudder" (James 2:19).

Jesus Christ

"Truth planted in the hearts of Socrates and Jesus grew and yielded the fruit of noble lives" (*New Age* [February 1943]: 100).

"No one Mason has the right to measure for another, within the walls of a Masonic Temple, the degree of veneration which he shall feel for any Reformer, or the Founder of any Religion" (Pike, *Morals and Dogma*, 22).

"It [Masonry] reverences all the great reformers. It sees in Moses, the Lawgiver of the Jews, in Confucius and Zoroaster, in Jesus of Nazareth, and in the Arabian Iconoclast, Great Teachers of Morality, and Eminent Reformers, if no more: and allows every brother of the Order to assign to each such higher and even Divine Character as his Creed and Truth require" (Pike, *Morals and Dogma*, 525).

"Whatever higher attributes the Founder of the Christian Faith may, in our belief, have had or not have had, none can deny that He taught and practiced a pure and elevated morality even at the risk and to the ultimate loss of his life" (Pike, *Morals and Dogma*, 308).

"It is not within the Providence of Masonry to determine how the ultimate triumph of Light and Truth and Good, over Darkness and Error and Evil, is to be achieved: nor whether the Redeemer, looked and longed for by all nations, hath appeared in Judea, or is yet to come" (Pike, *Morals and Dogma*, 525).

"Although he was a son, he learned obedience from what he suffered, and, once made perfect, he became the source of eternal salvation for all who obey him" (Heb. 5:8–9).

"Such a high priest meets our need— one who is holy, blameless, pure, set apart from sinners, exalted above the heavens" (Heb. 7:26).

"Therefore God exalted him [Jesus Christ] to the highest place and gave him the name that is above every name, that at the name of Jesus every knee should bow, in heaven and on earth and under the earth, and every tongue confess that Jesus Christ is Lord, to the glory of God the Father" (Phil. 2:9–11).

"God made him who had no sin to be sin for us, so that in him we might become the righteousness of God" (2 Cor. 5:21).

"He [Jesus] fell to the ground and prayed that if possible the hour might pass from him. 'Abba, Father,' he said, 'everything is possible for you. Take this cup from me. Yet not what I will, but what you will'" (Mark 14:35–36).

"He [Christ] has appeared once for all at the end of the ages to do away with sin by the sacrifice of himself" (Heb. 9:26).

The Doctrine of Human Nature and Sin

"Nor does Masonry teach that human nature is a depraved thing, like the ruin of a once proud building. Many think that man was once a perfect being but that through some unimaginable moral catastrophe he became corrupt into the last moral fibre of his being, so that, without some kind of supernatural or miraculous help from outside him he can never of himself do, or say, or think, or be aught but that which is deformed, vile and hideous. Those who hold to this kind of anthropology usually claim to know how supernatural help may be brought to bear on the corruption which is human nature, and they usually believe that only those who accept supernatural intervention according to their own formula have any hope whatever of escaping from the original sin into which every man is born." (Haywood, *The Great Teachings of Masonry,* 138– 39).

"The perfection is already within. All that is required is to remove the roughnesses and the excrescences, 'divesting our hearts and consciences of all devices and superfluities of life' to show forth the perfect man and Mason within. Thus the gavel becomes also the symbol of personal power" (Claudy, *Little Masonic Library* 4:51).

"Man also contains within him a life-force, a 'vital and immortal Principle' as Masonry calls it, which has not yet expanded to full development in him, and indeed in many men is scarcely active at all. Man, too, has that in him enabling him to evolve from the stage of the mortal animal to a being immortal, super-human, godlike.... Human evolution can be accelerated if not at present in the mass of humanity, yet in suitable individuals. Human nature is perfectible by an intensive process of purification and initiation" (Wilmhurst, *The Masonic Initiation,* 27–28).

"Sin entered the world through one man, and death through sin, and in this way death came to all men, because all sinned" (Rom. 5:12).

"All have sinned and fall short of the glory of God" (Rom. 3:23).

"Surely I was sinful at birth, sinful from the time my mother conceived me" (Ps. 51:5).

"I [Jesus] tell you the truth, no one can see the kingdom of God unless he is born again" (John 3:3).

"If we claim to be without sin, we deceive ourselves and the truth is not in us. If we confess our sins, he is faithful and just and will forgive us our sins and purify us from all unrighteousness. If we claim we have not sinned, we make him out to be a liar and his word has no place in our lives" (1 John 1:8–10).

"All of us have become like one who is unclean, and all our righteous acts are like filthy rags; we all shrivel up like a leaf, and like the wind our sins sweep us away" (Isa. 64:6).

"We know that the law is spiritual; but I am unspiritual, sold as a slave to sin. I do not understand what I do. For what I want to do I do not do, but what I hate I do" (Rom. 7:14 –15).

"We all, like sheep, have gone astray, each of us has turned to his own way" (Isa. 53:6).

47

Salvation

"If true religion is thus to be narrowed down to salvation in no other name under heaven, and St. Paul's words to this effect be understood in a spirit of bigoted literalness, then any such 'Christian' must indeed be straining his conscience to the breaking point by accepting initiation into the broader and deeper mysteries of Freemasonry. *I, for one, can never understand how anyone who takes an exclusive view of Christ as the only complete revelation of God's truth can become a Freemason without suffering from spiritual schizophrenia*" (Vindex, *Light Invisible*, 24–27 [emphasis added]).

"If any member of our fraternity acknowledges his faith in a Supreme Being, whose law is his guide, and strives honestly to live by his faith, we care not what the other articles of his creed may be, for we believe that when summoned from this sublunary abode, he will be received into the all-perfect, celestial lodge above, for he will, by his life, have made of earth the porch-way into heaven" (Thorpe, *Royal Arch*, n.p.).

Masonry "inculcates the practice of virtue but it applies no scheme of redemption for sin. It points its disciples to the path of righteousness" (Mackey, *Encyclopedia of Freemasonry*, 619).

"We find in the Masonic funeral service an allusion to a certain 'pass' whereby we may obtain entrance into the Grand Lodge above. What higher conception

"Salvation is found in no one else; for there is no other name under heaven given to men by which we must be saved" (Acts 4:12).

"No one can serve two masters. Either he will hate the one and love the other, or he will be devoted to the one and despise the other" (Matt. 6:24).

"If serving the LORD seems undesirable to you, then choose for yourselves this day whom you will serve. . . . But as for me and my household, we will serve the LORD" (Josh. 24:15).

"He who doubts is like a wave of the sea, blown and tossed by the wind. That man should not think he will receive anything from the Lord; he is a double-minded man, unstable in all he does" (James 1:6–8).

"For God so loved the world that he gave his one and only Son, *that whoever believes in him shall not perish* but have eternal life" (John 3:16).

"For they mouth empty, boastful words and, by appealing to the lustful desires of sinful human nature, they entice people who are just escaping from those who live in error. . . . If they have escaped the corruption of the world by knowing our Lord and Savior Jesus Christ and are again entangled in it and overcome, they are worse off at the end than they were at the beginning" (2 Peter 2:18, 20).

"Whoever believes in him is not condemned, but whoever does not believe stands condemned already because he has not believed in the name of God's one and only Son" (John 3:18).

"What shall we conclude then? Are we any better? Not at all! We have already made the charge that Jews and Gentiles alike are all under sin. As it is written:

could we have of the Master's Word than the pass whereby we can find immortality and entrance into the Grand Lodge on high? We are told that this pass is the pass of a pure and blameless life" (Ball, *The Builder,* 1:287).

"The one great God operating the universe has a place for every one of his sons whom he created. To think that Christians only merit immortality is narrow and not in keeping with the omnipotent love of the Creator of this vast universe" (*Masonic Inspiration* 1, no. 9 [July 1955]).

"Is Masonry anti-Christian? No, Masonry is not anti any religion. . . . Masonry encourages its members in their individual faiths. Masons do not oppose any faith" (Tresner, "Conscience and the Craft," *Scottish Rite Journal* [February 1993]): 17.

'There is no one righteous, not even one'" (Rom. 3:9–10).

"I am not ashamed of the gospel, because it is the power of God for the salvation of everyone who believes: first for the Jew, then for the Gentile. For in the gospel a righteousness from God is revealed, a righteousness that is by faith from first to last, just as it is written: 'The righteous will live by faith' " (Rom. 1:16–17).

"For it is by grace you have been saved, through faith—and this not from yourselves, it is the gift of God—not by works, so that no one can boast" (Eph. 2:8–9).

"What then shall we say that Abraham, our forefather, discovered in this matter? If, in fact, Abraham was justified by works, he had something to boast about—but not before God. What does the Scripture say? 'Abraham believed God, and it was credited to him as righteousness' " (Rom. 4:1–3).

"Do not let your hearts be troubled. Trust in God; trust also in me. . . . I am the way and the truth and the life. No one comes to the Father except through me" (John 14:1, 6).

"Elijah went before the people and said, 'How long will you waver between two opinions? If the *Lord* is God, follow him; but if Baal is God, follow him' " (1 Kings 18:21).

"We should not think that the divine being is like gold or silver or stone—an image made by man's design and skill. In the past God overlooked such ignorance, but now he commands all people everywhere to repent. For he has set a day when he will judge the world with justice by the man he has appointed. He has given proof of this to all men by raising him from the dead" (Acts 17:29–31).

49

The Occult

"Much light, it must be confessed, is thrown on many of the mystical names in the higher degrees by these dogmas of magic; and hence magic furnishes a curious and interesting study for the Freemason" (Mackey, *Encyclopedia of Freemasonry*, 459).

"Freemasonry and alchemy have sought the same results, the lesson of Divine Truth and the doctrine of immortal life, and they have both sought it by the same methods of symbolism. It is not, therefore, strange that in the eighteenth century, and perhaps before, we find an incorporation of much of the science of alchemy into that of Freemasonry" (Mackey, *Encyclopedia of Freemasonry*, 44).

"The Kaballa may be defined to be a system of philosophy which embraces certain mystical interpretations of Scripture, and metaphysical speculations concerning the Deity, man, and spiritual things. Much use is made of it in the high degrees, and entire rites have been constructed on its principles. Hence it demands a place in my general work on Masonry" (Mackey, *Encyclopedia of Freemasonry*, 375).

"Let no one be found among you who ... practices divination or sorcery, interprets omens, engages in witchcraft, or casts spells, or who is a medium or spiritist or who consults the dead" (Deut. 18:10–11; cf. Ex. 7; 8; Lev. 19:31; 1 Sam. 28).

"See to it that no one takes you captive through hollow and deceptive philosophy, which depends on human tradition and the basic principles of this world rather than on Christ" (Col. 2:8).

"Command certain men not to teach false doctrines any longer nor to devote themselves to myths and endless genealogies. These promote controversies rather than God's work—which is by faith" (1 Tim. 1:3–4).

"To suit their own desires, they will gather around them a great number of teachers to say what their itching ears want to hear. They will turn their ears away from the truth and turn aside to myths" (2 Tim. 4:3–4).

"We did not follow cleverly invented stories when we told you about the power and coming of our Lord Jesus Christ . . ." (2 Peter 1:16).

Oaths

"Mr. _____, upon entering the Lodge for the first time, receive you on the point of a sharp instrument pressing your naked left breast, which is to teach you, as this is an instrument of torture to your flesh, so should the recollection of it ever be to your mind and conscience should you attempt to reveal the secrets of Masonry unlawfully" (Whalen, *Handbook of Secret Organizations,* 57).

"... binding myself under no less penalty than that of having my throat cut from ear to ear, my tongue torn out by its roots and buried in the rough sands of the sea at low water mark where the tide ebbs and flows twice in twenty-four hours, should I ever knowingly or willingly violate this my solemn oath and obligation as an Entered Apprentice Mason. So help me God, and keep me steadfast in the due performance of the same" (*King Solomon and His Followers,* 22).

"You cannot cast away your stone. It is yourself. You cannot evade it and its responsibilities by resigning and remaining absent from the Brotherhood in which you first acquired the stone. Once a Mason, always a Mason: in this world and in worlds to come. You stand solemnly and eternally covenanted, not only to yourself and your Brotherhood, but to the Eternal Sacred Law, to proceed with your Masonic work to the end. That Law does not permit you to stultify an obligation deliberately made upon It, even if made ignorantly" (*King Solomon and His Followers,* 153).

"Come to me [Jesus], all you who are weary and burdened, and I will give you rest. Take my yoke upon you and learn from me, for I am gentle and humble in heart, and you will find rest for your souls. For my yoke is easy and my burden is light" (Matt 11:28–30).

"You shall not misuse the name of the LORD your God, for the LORD will not hold anyone guiltless who misuses his name" (Ex. 20:7).

"Above all, my brothers, do not swear— not by heaven or by earth or by anything else. Let your 'Yes' be yes, and your 'No,' no, or you will be condemned" (James 5:12).

"You have heard that it was said to the people long ago, 'Do not break your oath, but keep the oaths you have made to the Lord.' But I [Jesus] tell you, Do not swear at all: either by heaven, for it is God's throne; or by the earth, for it is his footstool; or by Jerusalem, for it is the city of the Great King. And do not swear by your head, for you cannot make even one hair white or black. Simply let your 'Yes' be 'Yes,' and your 'No,' 'No'; anything beyond this comes from the evil one" (Matt. 5:33–37).

51

Racism

"There are excellent reasons for this apparent race discrimination which only a Mason can fully understand; suffice it to say here that, feelings being what they are, that such a step would endanger the harmony of the lodge, which is a very primary consideration. Secondly, although Negroes today may technically fulfill the Masonic Requirement, being "free," their subordinate economic, educational, and cultural position is such that they hardly fulfill the spirit of that prerequisite to initiation" (Vindex, *Light Invisible*, 1952).*

"For God so loved the *world* that he gave his one and only Son, that *whoever* believes in him shall not perish but have eternal life" (John 3:16 [emphasis added]).

"You are all sons of God through faith in Christ Jesus, for all of you who were baptized into Christ have clothed yourselves with Christ. There is neither Jew nor Greek, slave nor free, male nor female, for you are all one in Christ Jesus" (Gal. 3:26–28).

Sources

Ball, *The Builder*

Carl H. Claudy, "A Master's Wage," *Little Masonic Library* 4 (Richmond, Va.: Macoy Publishing and Masonic Supply Co., 1946).

Harry L. Haywood, *The Great Teachings of Masonry,* rev. ed. (Richmond, Va.: Macoy Publishing and Masonic Supply Co., 1986).

King Solomon and His Followers, No. 2: Missouri (Richmond, Va.: Macoy Publishing and Masonic Supply Co., 1990).

Philip H. Lochhass, *Freemasonry in the Light of the Bible* (1954; reprint, St. Louis: Concordia Publishing House, 1976).

Albert G. Mackey, *Encyclopedia of Freemasonry,* 2 vols., rev. ed. (Chicago: Masonic History Co., 1946).

Masonic Inspiration 1, no. 9 (Morris Plains, N.J.: Charles Van Cott Publishers, July 1955).

New Age Magazine (various issues).

Albert Pike, *Morals and Dogma* (Charleston, S.C.: Supreme Council of the 33rd Degree for the Southern Jurisdiction, 1881).

Quarterly Bulletin (July 1915).

Thorpe, *Royal Arch.*

Jim Tresner, "Conscience and the Craft: Questions on Religion and Freemasonry," *Scottish Rite Journal* (February 1993).

Vindex, *Light Invisible: The Freemasonry Answer to Darkness Visible* (London: Britons Publishing Co., 1964).

Whalen, *Handbook of Secret Organizations.*

W. L. Wilmhurst, *The Masonic Initiation* (London: John M. Watkins, 1957).

---

*It should be noted that some modern Masons do indeed repudiate racism, but published statements to this effect are uncommon.

Chapter VII:
Mind Sciences

Author: Todd Ehrenborg; summary by Alan W. Gomes

Background

The "mind sciences" comprise several different cults that share a common philosophical outlook on God and the nature of reality. They are so named because they speak of God as "Divine Mind," an impersonal principle. Mind science groups teach that Divine Mind constitutes the whole of reality; the material world either does not exist or is otherwise an aspect of Divine Mind. Thus, mind science teaching is pantheistic (or sometimes panentheistic)—(see also the New Age Movement).

The three largest groups are considered here: Christian Science (CS), Religious Science (RS), and Unity School of Christianity (USC). CS was founded by Mary Baker Eddy in 1879. Her views are most particularly set forth in her *Science and Health with Key to the Scriptures.* "Metaphysical healing" was an important part of her teaching and is a crucial component of CS belief. At present there are about 250,000 Christian Scientists. RS (also known as Science of Mind) was founded by Ernest Holmes in 1927. His main work is entitled *Science of Mind.* RS boasts about 600,000 members and is the fastest-growing mind science cult. USC was founded by Charles and Myrtle Fillmore in the late 1800s. There are about 110,000 members in more than 300 churches worldwide.

Summary of Beliefs

Concerning **revelation,** USC and RS teach that truth is found in the "Bibles" of many religions—though it is taught most clearly and fully in their own group. These "Bibles"—including the Christian Bible—must be interpreted metaphysically. CS differs, claiming that "true Christianity" can only be understood through Eddy's *Science and Health.* **God** is seen as Divine Mind: impersonal yet individual. God, "It," is a triply divine Principle or Mind: Life, Truth, and Love. God is "All-in-all." Everything in the universe is a unified Whole, expressed as "all is one." CS denies the existence of the **material world;** it is illusory. RS and USC, by contrast, affirm the reality of the matter, but say that the material universe is God's Body; he is in everything but greater than everything (panentheism).

Jesus was merely a human man, a divine idea (or an idea of God) in corporeal form. Jesus was the Son of God but not God the Son (as Trinitarians affirm). Jesus was not the Christ; rather, "Christ" refers to "the divine manifestation of God, which comes to the flesh to destroy incarnate error." RS specifically affirms that Jesus became the Christ, as all people can become. According to RS, the Christ is the Higher Self of every individual. All mind science groups teach that Jesus is our Way-shower to salvation, but he cannot save us. Jesus was a master metaphysician who taught the truths of Divine Science. His teachings must be interpreted metaphysically.

Human beings are perfect, without sin (since sin is unreal), and eternal. They are part of God. RS and USC teach that man's body—like all other matter—is a manifestation of Divine Mind. Concerning **Christ's death and resurrection,** since death is an illusion, Christ did not die on the cross. Consequently, bodily resurrection was and is unnecessary. **Sin,** matter, evil, disease and death are unreal and an illusion; they are merely destructive forms of thought. Man already has everlasting **salvation;** there is no final judgment. "Salvation" is being saved from the error that sin, sickness, and death exist. People must overcome their ignorance and realize that they are already one with God. Additionally, CS asserts that there is no way into the kingdom of heaven except through the practice of CS.

Unique to USC is the teaching of **reincarnation.** After bodily death, the soul falls asleep until its next incarnation. Successive rebirths take the form of another human being. Each incarnation is to work out one's "karma" and to progress to the next level of existence, eventually culminating in eternal life.

Parallel Comparison Chart

Mind Sciences	The Bible
God	
[CS] "The Scriptures imply that God is All-in-all. From this it follows that nothing possesses reality nor existence except the divine Mind and His ideas" (*S/H*, 331).	"In the beginning you laid the foundations of the earth, and the heavens are the *work of your hands*. They will *perish*, but you remain; they will all wear out like a garment" (Ps. 102:25–26).* [God is distinct from his creation.]
[RS] "The whole universe is the manifestation of a Unity which men call God" (*What Religious Science Teaches*, 12).	"It is I who *made the earth* and *created mankind upon it*. My own hands *stretched out* the heavens; I marshaled their starry hosts" (Isa. 45:12). [God is distinct from his creation.]
[USC] "Each rock, tree, animal, everything visible, is a manifestation of the one Spirit—God—differing only in degree of manifestation; and each of the numberless modes of manifestation, or	"They exchanged the truth of God for a lie, and worshiped and served created

*Italics in the text of either column in this parallel comparison chart have breen added for emphasis and are not in the original works cited.

individualities, however insignificant, contains the whole" (Cady, *Lessons in Truth*, 8).

[RS] "God is not a person, God is a Presence personified in us" (*S/M*, 308).

[USC] "The Father is Principle. The Son is that Principle revealed in the creative plan. The Holy Spirit is the executive power of both Father and Son carrying out the creative plan" (*MBD*, 629).

[USC] "God is not a being or person, having life, intelligence, love, power. God is perfect love and infinite power. God is the total of these, the total of all good" (*Lessons in Truth*, 6).

[CS] "Man originated not from dust, materially, but from Spirit, spiritually" (*Misc. Writ.*, 57). "Man is not matter; he is not made up of brain, blood, bones, and other material elements.... Man is spiritual and perfect.... Man is idea, the image, of Love; he is not physique" (*S/H*, 475).

[RS] "There is that within *every* individual which partakes of the nature of the Universal Wholeness and—in so far as it operates *is God*. That is the meaning of Immanuel, the meaning of the word Christ. There is that within us which partakes of the nature of the Divine Being, and since it partakes of the nature of the Divine Being, we are divine" (*S/M*, 33–34).

[USC] "So we say that each individual manifestation of God contains the whole; not for a moment meaning that each individual is God in His entirety, so to speak, but that each is God come forth, shall I say? in different quantity or degree" (Cady, *Lessons in Truth*, 9).

things rather than the Creator" (Rom. 1:25).

"But the Egyptians are men and *not God*; their horses are *flesh and not spirit*" (Isa. 31:3).

"God is in heaven and you are on earth" (Eccl. 5:2).

"And a voice from heaven said, 'This is my Son, whom I love; with him I am well pleased.'" (Matt 3:17). [This shows a personal subject-object relationship.]

"The LORD God formed man from the dust of the ground and breathed into his nostrils the breath of life, and man became a living being" (Gen. 2:7).

"Know that the LORD is God. It is he who has made us, and we are his; we are his people, the sheep of his pasture" (Ps. 100:3).

"God is not a man, that he should lie, nor a son of man, that he should change his mind" (Num. 23:19).

"When the crowd saw what Paul had done, they shouted, . . . 'The gods have come down to us in human form!' But when the apostles Barnabas and Paul heard of this, they tore their clothes and rushed out into the crowd, shouting: 'Men, why are you doing this? *We too are only men, human like you.* We are bringing you good news, telling you to turn from these worthless things *to the living God, who made heaven and earth and sea and everything in them*" (Acts 14:11, 14–15).

Jesus Christ

[CS] "The Christian who believes in the First Commandment is a monotheist. Thus he virtually unites with the Jew's belief in one God, and recognizes that *Jesus Christ is not God*, as Jesus himself declared, but is the Son of God" (*S/H*, 361).

[RS] "Jesus never thought of himself as different from others" (*S/M*, 361). "Mental Science does not deny the divinity of Jesus; but it does affirm the divinity of all people. It does not deny that Jesus was the son of God; but it affirms that all men are the sons of God" (*S/M*, 161–62).

[USC] "The difference between Jesus and us is not one of inherent spiritual capacity, but in difference of demonstration of it. Jesus was potentially perfect, and He expressed that perfection; we are potentially perfect, and we have not yet expressed it" (*What Unity Teaches*, 3).

[CS] "Jesus is the human man, and Christ is the divine idea; hence the duality of Jesus the Christ" (*S/H*, 473).

[RS] "JESUS—the name of a man. Distinguished from the Christ. . . . Christ is not limited to any person, nor does He appear in only one age" (*S/M*, 603, 363).

[USC] "By Christ is not meant the man Jesus" (*Unity Magazine*, no. 2, p. 146).

"You are from *below*, I am from *above*; you are of *this world*, I am *not of this world*. I said therefore to you, that you shall die in your sins; for unless you believe that *I am He*, you shall die in your sins. . . . Truly, truly, I say to you, before Abraham was born, I am'" (John 8:23–24, 58 NASB). [Jesus takes the divine name of *I am* (YHWH, Jehovah) from Exodus 3:14 for himself.]

"'*I and the Father are one*.' Again the Jews picked up stones to stone him, but Jesus said to them, 'I have shown you many great miracles from the Father. For which of these do you stone me?' 'We are not stoning you for any of these,' replied the Jews, 'but for blasphemy, because you, a mere man, *claim to be God*'" (John 10:30–33; cf. 5:18).

"For in Christ all the fullness of the Deity lives in bodily form" (Col. 2:9).

"'Are you the Christ, the Son of the Blessed One?' '*I am*,' said Jesus" (Mark 14:61–62).

"'Who do you say that I am?' Simon Peter answered, '*You are the Christ*, the Son of the Living God.' Jesus replied, 'Blessed are you Simon son of Jonah, for this was *not revealed to you by man, but by my Father in heaven*'" (Matt. 16:15–17).

Death and Resurrection

[CS] "Jesus' students, not sufficiently advanced fully to understand their Master's triumph, did not perform many wonderful works, until they saw him after his crucifixion and learned that he had *not died*" (*S/H*, 45–46). "RESURRECTION. Spiritualization of thought; a new and higher idea of immortality, or spiritual existence; material belief yielding to spiritual understanding" (*S/H*, 593).

[RS] "The resurrection is the death of the belief that we are separated from God. For death is to the illusion alone and not to Reality. God did not die. What happened was that man awoke to Life. The awakening must be on the part of man since God already is Life" (*S/M*, 413).

[USC] "We believe that we do free our minds and resurrect our bodies by true thoughts and words and that this resurrection is being carried forward daily and will ultimate in a final purification of the body from all earthly errors. Through this process we shall be raised to the consciousness of continuous health and eternal life here and now, following Jesus Christ in the regeneration or 'new birth'" (*Unity's Statement of Faith*, Art. 28).

"Jesus called out with a loud voice, 'Father, into your hands I commit my spirit.' When he had said this, he breathed his last" (Luke 23:46).

"But when they came to Jesus and found that he was already dead, they did not break his legs" (John 19:33).

"He humbled himself and became obedient to death—even death on a cross!" (Phil 2:8).

"And if the Spirit of him who raised Jesus from the dead is living in you, he who raised Christ from the dead will also give life to your mortal bodies through his Spirit, who lives in you" (Rom. 8:11).

"And if *Christ has not been raised*, our preaching is useless and so is your faith. More than that, we are then found to be false witnesses about God, for we have testified about God that he *raised Christ from the dead*. And if Christ has not been *raised*, your faith is futile; you are *still in your sins*" (1 Cor. 15:14–15, 17).

"Jesus answered them, 'Destroy this temple, and I will raise it again in three days.' But the temple he had spoken of was his *body*" (John 2:19, 21). [Body = Greek: *soma* = physical body.]

Sin

[CS] "In Science there is no fallen state of being; for therein is no inverted image of God, no escape from the focal radiation of the Infinite" (*No and Yes*, p. 17). "Christ came to destroy the belief of sin" (*S/H*, 473). "The way to escape the misery of sin is to cease sinning. There is no other way" (*S/H*, 327).

"Therefore, just as *sin entered* the world through one man, and death through sin, and in this way *death came to all men*, because *all sinned*—for before the law was given, sin was in the world" (Rom. 5:12–13).

"Christ Jesus came into the world to save sinners—of whom I am the worst" (1 Tim. 1:15).

Sin (cont.)

[RS] "SIN—We have tried to show that there is no sin but a mistake, and no punishment but a consequence. The Law of cause and effect. Sin is merely missing the mark. God does not punish sin. As we correct our mistakes, we forgive our own sins" (*S/M*, 633).

[USC] "The 'eternal sin,' or unpardonable sin, . . . is the belief that God is the creator of disease or inharmony of any nature. . . . Man's sins are forgiven when he ceases to sin and opens his mind to the fact that he is heir only to the good" (*MBD*, 620).

[USC] "The inharmonies in the world can be eliminated by eliminating them from man's mind. This can be done by understanding that God's creation is all that there is and knowing it to be good" (*MBD*, 158).

"If we claim to be without sin, we *deceive* ourselves and the truth is not in us. *If we confess our sins*, he is faithful and just to forgive us our sins and purify us from all unrighteousness, *If we claim we have not sinned*, we make him out to be a *liar* and his word has no place in our lives" (1 John 1:8–10).

"Yet he [the Lord] does not leave the guilty unpunished" (Ex. 34:7).

"*Everything* that does not come from faith is *sin*" (Rom. 14:23).

"Everyone who sins breaks the law; in fact, sin is lawlessness" (1 John 3:4).

"The wages of sin is death" (Rom. 6:23).

Salvation

[CS] "Salvation—Life, Truth, and Love understood and demonstrated as supreme over all; sin, sickness, and death destroyed" (*S/H*, 593). "This salvation means: Saved from error, or error overcome" (*Misc. Writ.*, 89). "Final deliverance from error, whereby we rejoice in immortality, boundless freedom, and sinless sense, is not reached through paths of flowers nor by pinning one's faith without works to another's vicarious effort" (*S/H*, 22). "Man as God's idea is already saved with an everlasting salvation" (*Misc. Writ.*, 261).

[RS] "SALVATION—is not a thing, not an end, but a Way. The Way of Salvation is through man's unity with the Whole. Grace is the givingness of Spirit to Its Creation" (*S/M*, 631).

"Since we have now been justified *by his blood*, how much more shall we be saved from God's wrath through him! For if, when *we were God's enemies*, we were *reconciled to him through the death of his Son*, how much more, having been reconciled, shall we be saved through his life!" (Rom. 5:9–10).

"He himself *bore our sins* in *his body* on the tree, so that we might die to sins and live for righteousness; *by his wounds* you have been healed" (1 Peter 2:24; cf. Isa. 53:4–12).

"*Believe* in the Lord Jesus, and *you will* be saved" (Acts 16:31).

"If you confess with your mouth, '*Jesus is Lord*,' and *believe in your heart* that God raised him from the *dead*, you will be saved" (Rom. 10:9).

"We believe that the ultimate goal of life to be a complete emancipation from all discord of every nature, and that this goal is sure to be attained by all" (*What RS Teaches*, 50).

[USC] "Being 'born-again' or 'born from above' is not a miraculous change that takes place in man; it is the establishment of that which has always existed as the perfect man idea of divine Mind" (*Christian Healing*, 24).

"For it is *by grace* you have been saved, *through faith*—and this *not from yourselves*, it is the *gift* of God—*not of works*, so that no one can boast" (Eph. 2:8–9, cf. Titus 3:5–7).

"I tell you the truth, *unless* a man is born of water and the Spirit, he cannot enter the kingdom of God. Flesh gives birth to flesh, but the Spirit gives birth to spirit" (John 3:5, 6).

Doctrine of Revelation

[CS] "The material record of the Bible ... is no more important to our well being than the history of Europe and America" (*Misc. Writ.*, 170). "The Scriptures cannot properly be interpreted in a literal way.... the literal rendering of the Scriptures makes them nothing valuable, but often is the foundation of unbelief and hopelessness" (*Misc. Writ.*, 169).

[RS] "The Science of Mind is not a special revelation of any individual; it is, rather, the culmination of all revelations" (*S/M*, 35).

"REVELATION— ... Since the mind that man uses is the same Mind that God uses, the One and Only Mind, the avenues of Revelation can never be closed. But no man can receive the Revelation for another" (*S/M*, 630).

[USC] "Scripture may be a satisfactory authority for those who are not themselves in direct communion with the Lord" (*Unity Magazine*, no.7, Oct. 1896, p. 400). "Spiritual principle is embodied in the sacred books of the world's living religions. Christians ... believe that the

"Sanctify them by the truth; your word is truth" (John 17:17). [Jesus speaking to the Father.]

"The Scripture cannot be broken" (John 10:35).

"All Scripture is God-breathed and is useful for teaching, rebuking, correcting, and training in righteousness" (2 Tim. 3:16).

"We do not use deception, *nor do we distort the word of God*. On the contrary, *by setting forth the truth plainly* we commend ourselves to every man's conscience in the sight of God" (2 Cor. 4:2).

"Contend for the faith that was *once for all* entrusted to the saints" (Jude 3).

"To the law and to the testimony! If they do not speak according to this word, they have no light of dawn" (Isa. 8:20).

"*Every word* of God is *flawless*.... Do not add to his words*, or he will rebuke you and prove you a liar" (Prov. 30:5–6; cf. Rev. 22:18–19; Deut. 4:2).

Doctrine of Revelation (cont.)

Bible is the greatest and most keenly spiritual of all Scriptures, though they realize that other Scriptures such as the *Zend-Avesta* and the *Upanishads*, as well as the teachings of Buddha, the *Koran*, and the *Tao of Lao-tse* and the writings of Confucius, contain expressions of eminent spiritual truths ..." (*What Unity Teaches*, 4).

Reincarnation Versus Resurrection

[USC] "We believe that the dissolution of spirit, soul, and body, caused by death, is annulled by rebirth of the same spirit and soul in another body here on earth. We believe the repeated incarnations of man to be a merciful provision of our loving Father to the end that all may have opportunity to attain immortality through regeneration, as did Jesus" (*Unity's Statement of Faith*, Art. 22).

[USC] "Reincarnation replaces the old belief in condemnation and damnation by the faith of the everlasting mercy and forgiveness of God. Neither does our heavenly Father condemn or punish His children" (*Reincarnation*, 3).

[USC] "Reincarnation gives to the soul and spirit of man who sins or makes mistakes repeated opportunities, until he learns to live in conformity with God's law. When man learns to live and apply the truth as did Jesus Christ then the necessity for reincarnation will be done away with. He will have learned to live without dying.... The goal of man is eternal life, and in each incarnation that goal is brought nearer" (*Reincarnation*, 5, 8).

"Then Christ would have had to suffer many times since the creation of the world. But now he has appeared *once for all* at the end of the ages *to do away with sin by the sacrifice of himself*. Just as man is destined to *die once*, and *after that to face judgment*, so *Christ was sacrificed once to take away the sins of many people*; and he will appear a second time, not to bear sin, but *to bring salvation* to those who are waiting for him" (Heb. 9:26–28).

"We are confident, I say, and would prefer to be *away from the body and at home with the Lord*. For *we must all appear before the judgment seat of Christ*, that each one may receive what is due him for the things done in the body, whether good or bad" (2 Cor. 5:8, 10). [For the believer, to be absent from the body means to be present with the Lord.]

"Then he will say to those on his left, 'Depart from me, you who are cursed, into the eternal fire prepared for the devil and his angels.' Then they will go away to *eternal* punishment, but the righteous to *eternal* life" (Matt. 25:41, 46).

Sources

Christian Science
> Mary Baker Eddy, *Miscellaneous Writings* (Boston: CS Publishing Society, 1896).
> Mary Baker Eddy, *No and Yes,* (N.p.: 1891).
> Mary Baker Eddy, *Science and Health with Key to the Scriptures,* 1971 ed. (Boston: CS Publishing Society, 1971).

Religious Science
> Ernest Holmes, *The Science of Mind* (New York: Dodd, Mead, 1965).
> Ernest Holmes, *What Religious Science Teaches*(Los Angeles: Science of Mind Publications, 1974).

Unity School of Christianity
> H. Emilie Cady, *Lessons in Truth* (Kansas City: Unity School of Christianity, 1941).
> Charles Fillmore, *Christian Healing* (Unity Village, Mo.: Unity School of Christianity, 1939).
> James D. Freeman, *The Case for Reincarnation* (Unity Village, MO.: Unity School of Christianity, 1986).
> *Metaphysical Bible Dictionary* (Kansas City: Unity School of Christianity, 1942).
> Elizabeth Sand Turner, *What Unity Teaches* (Unity Village, Mo.: Unity School of Christianity, n.d.).
> *Unity, a Magazine devoted to Christian Healing* (various issues).
> Unity's Statement of Faith.

Chapter VIII:
New Age Movement

Author: Ron Rhodes; summary by Alan W. Gomes

Background

The New Age movement is defined as "a loosely structured network of individuals and organizations who share a vision of a new age of enlightenment and harmony (the 'Age of Aquarius') and who subscribe to a common 'worldview.'" This worldview entails the ideas that all is one (monism), that all is God (pantheism), and that people can experience this oneness with the divine (mysticism). The New Age movement (NAM) is highly diverse and decentralized. There is no person, group of people, or organization that speaks for it, much less a well-organized, orchestrated conspiracy. Rather, because of their shared core philosophy, New Agers cooperate to varying degrees and in varying ways to promote their common interests.

The NAM is highly eclectic and syncretistic, meaning that New Agers draw from various and varied sources of "truth," combining different (and often contradictory) elements into their beliefs. The New Age philosophy has made inroads, some significant, into many different areas of life, including health care (such as "holistic health"), psychology (the human potential movement), science (New Age "physics"), politics (one-world government), education (centering, confluent education, guided imagery), and business (the human potential movement). Because of the movement's diversity, the number of New Age practitioners is impossible to determine. There are more than three thousand publishers of New Age and occult books, journals, and magazines. Major publishers such as Bantam and Ballantine have New Age divisions. Some best-selling New Age books include *A Course in Miracles* and Shirley MacLaine's *Out on a Limb*.

Summary of Beliefs

New Agers believe that the **Bible** contains hidden, secret, esoteric meanings, especially in the teachings of Jesus. The Bible, when properly understood, supports the New Age worldview (all is one, all is God, and man is God). Concerning **revelation,** New Agers believe that Jesus is one of many enlightened individuals who have revealed God's truth to humanity. The revelations from the various world's religions and great religious teachers all affirm the New Age truths of pantheism, monism, and human divinity. Revelations may also come today from a variety of extradimensional beings, including disembodied humans (such as ascended masters). These revelations are typically "channeled" through an individual who becomes controlled by the spiritual entity revealing the information.

Concerning **God,** New Agers hold to a pantheistic conception. That is, God is all and all is God. God is not seen as personal but is variously described as an impersonal Force, or Cosmic Consciousness, or Energy. Regarding **Jesus Christ,** some New Agers make a sharp distinction between Jesus and the Christ. "Jesus" refers to the literal man Jesus, while "the Christ" is often (though not always) defined as a cosmic, divine entity that indwelt the man Jesus. Some New Agers also teach that Jesus went East and attained enlightenment through the teaching of Eastern gurus. Thus enlightened, Jesus became a "way-shower," much as other holy men (such as Buddha, Krishna et al.). In their doctrine of **man,** New Agers affirm human divinity. Since all is God (pantheism) and all is one (monism), it follows that man—like everything else—is part of this divine oneness. Being God, man has unlimited potential and can even create his own reality.

Salvation in New Age thinking is unnecessary. Since New Agers deny the concept of sin, there is no need to be saved from it. It also follows that Jesus Christ could not have atoned for sin. People are not hindered in life by sin but by failing to recognize their own divinity—hence the need for enlightenment, not salvation. New Agers typically affirm the doctrine of **reincarnation,** through which a person is ultimately reunited with God.

Parallel Comparision Chart

New Age	The Bible

Continuing Revelation

"Never has there been a time, cycle, or world period when there was not the giving out of the teaching and spiritual help which human need demanded" (Bailey, *The Reappearance of the Christ,* 147).	"Dear friends ... I felt I had to write and urge you to contend for *the faith* that was *once for all* entrusted to the saints" (Jude 3).

Esoteric Interpretation of Scripture

"The greatest teachers of divinity agree that nearly all ancient books [including the Bible] were written symbolically and in a language intelligible only to the initiated" (cited in Sire, *Scripture Twisting,* 108).	"We do not use deception, *nor do we distort the word of God.* On the contrary, by *setting forth the truth plainly* we commend ourselves to every man's conscience in the sight of God" (2 Cor. 4:2).

God

"God is the sum total of all that exists in the whole of the manifested and un-manifested universe" (Creme, *The Reappearance of the Christ*, 115).

"The nations of the earth see God from different points of view, and so he does not seem the same to everyone.... You Brahmans call him Parabrahm; in Egypt he is Thoth; and Zeus is his name in Greece; Jehovah is his Hebrew name" (Dowling, *The Aquarian Gospel*, 56).

"There is not one place, one thing, one time that does not include his presence. God is the life within all things. He contains all things" (D. Spangler, *Revelation*, 150).

"It is I who *made* the earth and *created* mankind upon it. My own hands *stretched out* the heavens; I *marshaled* their starry hosts" [God is distinct from the creation] (Isa. 45:12).

"Who among the gods is like you, O LORD[Jehovah]? Who is like you—majestic in holiness, awesome in glory, working wonders?" (Ex. 15:11).

"Who is like the LORD our God [Jehovah], the One who sits enthroned on high, who stoops down to look on the heavens and the earth?" (Ps. 113:5–6).

"God is *in heaven* and you are *on earth*" (Eccl. 5:2).

"They exchanged the truth of God for a lie, and worshiped and served created things rather than the Creator—who is forever praised. Amen" (Rom. 1:25).

Humanity Is God

"I think the whole purpose of life is to reown the Godlikeness within us; the perfect love, the perfect wisdom, the perfect understanding" (Galyean, in "Educators Look East," 29).

"You are God. You know you are Divine. But you must continually remember your Divinity and, most important, act accordingly" (MacLaine, *Out on a Limb*, 209).

[Yahweh speaking] "See now that I myself am He! *There is no god besides me.* I put to death and I bring to life, I have wounded and I will heal, and no one can deliver out of my hand" (Deut. 32:39).

"You shall have no other gods before me" (Ex. 20:3).

"On the appointed day Herod, wearing his royal robes, sat on his throne and delivered a public address to the people. They shouted, 'This is the voice of a god, not of a man.' Immediately, because Herod did not give praise to God, an angel of the Lord struck him down, and he was eaten by worms and died" (Acts 12:21–23).

"We are all part of God. We are all individualized reflections of the God source. God is us and we are God" (MacLaine, *Dancing in the Light*, 354).

[Yahweh speaking] "I will send the full force of my plagues against you and against your officials and your people, so you may know that *there is no one like me in all the earth*" (Ex. 9:14, italics added).

Sin

"The tragedy of the human race was that we had forgotten we were each Divine" [i.e., there is no *sin*, just *ignorance*] (MacLaine, *Dancing in the Light*, 347).

"There is no evil—only the lack of knowledge" (MacLaine, *Dancing in the Light*, 259).

"Until mankind realizes that there is, in truth, no good and there is, in truth, no evil, there will be no peace" (MacLaine, *Dancing in the Light*, 357).

"If we claim to be without sin, we deceive ourselves and the truth is not in us" (1 John 1:8).

"Dear friend, do not imitate *what is evil* but *what is good*. Anyone who does *what is good* is from God. Anyone who does *what is evil* has not seen God" (3 John 11, italics added).

Salvation

"Your thoughts are always creating your reality—it's up to you to take charge of your thoughts and consciously create a reality that is fulfilling" [self-salvation] (Gershon and Straub, *Empowerment*, 21).

"You are unlimited. You just don't realize it" [no need of salvation from sin] (MacLaine, *Dancing in the Light*, 133).

"For it is by grace you have been saved, through faith—and this *not from yourselves*, it is the gift of God— *not by works*, so that no one can boast" (Eph. 2:8–9).

"All of us have become like one who is unclean, and all our righteous acts are like filthy rags; we all shrivel up like a leaf, and like the wind our sins sweep us away" (Isa. 64:6).

Reincarnation

"Reincarnation is like show business. You just keep doing it until you get it right" (MacLaine, *Out on a Limb*, 233).

"Man is destined to die once, and after that to face judgment" (Heb. 9:27).

65

Jesus

"Jesus was one of a line of spiritual teachers, a line that continues today" (D. Spangler, *Reflections on the Christ,* 28).

"Jesus, Buddha, Zoroaster, Lao Tse, Muhammad and many others known and unknown to history are representatives of divinely anointed individuals representing part of the goal for the human race" (J. Spangler, "Compass Points," 4).

"To my way of thinking, the Christian Churches have released into the world a view of the Christ which is impossible for modern people to accept: as the one and only Son of God, sacrificed by a loving Father to save us from the results of our sins—a blood sacrifice, straight out of the old Jewish dispensation" (Creme, *The Reappearance of the Christ,* 47).

Jesus answered, "I am the way and the truth and the life. *No one comes to the Father except through me*" (John 14:6, italics added).

"Salvation is found in *no one else,* for there is *no other name* under heaven given to men by which we must be saved" (Acts 4:12, italics added).

"For there is one God and *one mediator* between God and men, the man Christ Jesus" (1 Tim. 2:5, italics added).

"This is my *blood* of the covenant, which is *poured out for many for the forgiveness of sins*" (Matt. 26:28, italics added).

"For you know that it was not with perishable things such as silver or gold that you were *redeemed* from the empty way of life handed down to you from your forefathers, but with the *precious blood of Christ, a lamb without blemish or defect*" (1 Peter 1:18–19, italics added).

The Second Coming

"To the Christians he will be the second coming of Christ, to the Jews the Messiah, the Imam Mahdi to the Muslims, Krishna to the Hindus, and to the Buddhists he will be the fifth Buddha" (Miller, "Benjamin Creme and the Reappearance," 3, 7).

"The Second Coming is occurring now in the hearts and minds of millions of individuals of all faiths as they come to realize this spiritual presence within themselves and each other." (D. Spangler, *Cooperation with the Spirit,* 4).

[Angels speaking to disciples] "Men of Galilee," they said, "why do you stand here looking into the sky? *This same Jesus,* who has been taken from you into heaven, *will come back in the same way you have seen him go into heaven*" (Acts 1:11, italics added).

"Immediately after the distress of those days 'the sun will be darkened, and the moon will not give its light; the stars will fall from the sky, and the heavenly bodies will be shaken.' At that time the sign of the Son of Man will appear in the sky, and all the nations of the earth will mourn. They will see the Son of Man

"The second coming of the Christ in our age will be fundamentally, most importantly, a mass coming. It will be the manifestation of a consciousness within the multitudes" (D. Spangler, *Towards a Planetary Vision*, 108).

coming on the clouds of the sky, with power and great glory" (Matt. 24:29–30).

"Look, he is coming with the clouds, and every eye will see him, even those who pierced him; and all the peoples of the earth will mourn because of him. So shall it be! Amen" (Rev. 1:7).

"On his robe and on his thigh he has this name written: KING OF KINGS AND LORD OF LORDS" (Rev. 19:16).

Sources

Alice A. Bailey, *The Reappearance of the Christ* (New York: Lucis, 1948).

Benjamin Creme, *The Reappearance of the Christ and the Masters of Wisdom* (Los Angeles: Tara Center, 1980).

Levi Dowling, *The Aquarian Gospel of Jesus the Christ* (Santa Monica, Calif.: DeVorss, 1907).

Beverly Galyean, interview by Frances Adeney, "Educators Look East," *SCP Journal* (Winter 1981).

David Gershon and Gail Straub, *Empowerment: The Art of Creating Your Life as You Want It* (New York: Dell, 1989).

Shirley MacLaine, *Out on a Limb* (New York: Bantam, 1983).

Shirley MacLaine, *Dancing in the Light* (New York: Bantam, 1985).

Eliot Miller, "Benjamin Creme and the Reappearance of the Christ," *Forward* 6, no. 1.

James Sire, *Scripture Twisting* (Downers Grove, Ill.: InterVarsity Press, 1980).

David Spangler, *Cooperation with the Spirit* (Middleton, Wis.: Lorian Press, 1982).

David Spangler, *Reflections on the Christ* (Forres, Scotland: Findhorn, 1981).

David Spangler, *Revelation: The Birth of a New Age* (Middleton, Wis.: Lorian Press, 1976).

David Spangler, *Towards a Planetary Vision* (Forres, Scotland: Findhorn, 1977).

Julia Spangler, "Compass Points," *Lorian Journal* 1, no. 2.

Chapter IX:
Goddess Worship, Witchcraft and Neo-Paganism

Author: Craig S. Hawkins; summary by Alan W. Gomes

Background

Neo-paganism is the revival of the old gods and goddesses of pre-Christian polytheistic mythologies, mystery cults, and nature religions, such as those of the Celts, the Greeks, the Egyptians, the Romans, and the Sumerians. Neo-paganism also includes Native American Indian religions and shamanism as well as newly crafted religions based on avant-garde science fiction and fantasy works (such as the Church of All Worlds). Witchcraft is one form of Neo-paganism.

Neo-pagan beliefs are diverse, but certain common themes emerge. All Neo-pagans have an occultic worldview, in which magic plays a key role. Often the worship of the (or a) Goddess (or other entities, however understood) is of central importance. Precise statistics on the number of witches and Neo-pagans is difficult to ascertain. Estimates range from a low of 50,000 to upwards of 400,000 worldwide. Increased literature distribution suggests that the movement may be growing. Witchcraft should be carefully distinguished from satanism (see below), even though they are often lumped together in the popular imagination.

Summary of Beliefs

Concerning **truth and revelation,** Neo-pagans greatly disdain centralized external authorities and eschew precise doctrinal statements. Rather, they emphasize personal, subjective experiences and receive revelation through a variety of divinatory techniques. Many Neo-pagans simply ignore **Jesus Christ,** while others claim that he was himself a witch, or at least adept in the occultic arts. There are many beliefs concerning **God.** Some Neo-pagans are polytheists, some are pantheists ("all is God and God is all"), some are panentheists (the world is a manifestation of, or contained in, the divine), and some hold to combinations of these and other beliefs. Many witches believe in a variety of gods, goddesses, and other spiritual entities (such as fairies).

The worship and invocation of the **Goddess** plays a central role for many witches. For them, the earth is a (or the) manifestation of the Goddess.

Accordingly, they revere the earth and all life on it as sacred. For others, worship of the Goddess is balanced with reverence for the Horned God (most commonly known as Pan). Through various **magic** practices and rituals a witch can become "possessed" by, for example, the Goddess; the witch then becomes a conduit through whom the Goddess can speak and channel information. (Possession by the Goddess is known as "drawing down the moon.")

Neo-pagans believe that **human beings** are divine, or at least potentially so. They affirm that people are basically good. Neo-pagans do not believe in **sin** in the orthodox Christian sense. Rather, they speak of being "unbalanced" or out of harmony with Mother Earth, the Goddess, etc. Not surprisingly, Neo-pagans do not believe in **salvation** in the Christian sense, either, and they reject as arrogant Christian "exclusivism"—the notion of salvation only in Jesus Christ. While Neo-pagans do not believe in the biblical **heaven,** they do not believe that physical death spells the end of one's existence. After death, many hope to go to Summerland (or simply the Otherworld), a state of disembodied existence in which the soul is refreshed. Spirits in the Otherworld are available for contact through spiritism, necromancy, or divination. Many Neo-pagans do believe in some form of **reincarnation,** in which the souls in the Otherworld are born again on a physical plane. Reincarnation is seen to help facilitate one's spiritual evolution.

Parallel Comparison Chart

Neo-Pagans	The Bible
Revelation	
"In witchcraft, each of us must reveal our own truth" (Starhawk, *Spiral Dance*, 9).	"The secret things belong to the LORD our God, but the things revealed belong to us and to our children forever, that we may follow all the words of this law" (Deut. 29:29).
"Belief" has never seemed very relevant to the experiences and processes of the groups that call themselves, collectively, the Neo-Pagan movement" (Adler, *Drawing Down the Moon*, 20).	"All Scripture is God-breathed and is useful for teaching, rebuking, correcting and training in righteousness, so that the man of God may be thoroughly equipped for every good work" (2 Tim. 3:16).
"What little we know of the Mysteries seems to indicate that these rites emphasized (as the Craft, at its best, does today) *experience* as opposed to *dogma*, and *metaphor* and *myth* as opposed to doctrine.... Neither emphasizes theology, belief, or the written word" (Adler, *Drawing Down the Moon*, 441, emphasis in original).	"In the past God spoke to our forefathers through the prophets at many times and in various ways, but in these last days he has spoken to us by his Son" (Heb. 1:1–2).

69

Revelation (cont.)

"Since Paganism allows for individual expression and mythological preference, there will perhaps never be a set of codified traditions" (Jones and Matthews, *Voices from the Circle,* 32).

God

"[Neo-]Pagans recognize the divinity of Nature and of all living things" (Jones and Matthews, *Voices from the Circle,* 40).

"The followers of Wicca might well be considered 'duotheists'" (Adler, *Drawing Down the Moon,* 35).

"Divinity is immanent in all Nature" (Adler, *Drawing Down the Moon,* ix).

"All things in the universe are manifestations of Divinity, and as such are held to be sacred and venerable. The Gods are both immanent beings and parts of a transcendent whole" (Paul Suliin).

"It [witchcraft] is monotheistic because it is based on an underlying belief in One Life Force, One Power overall, One Essence or One Energy Source of the Universe. But witchcraft also qualifies as pagan because it acknowledges two primary aspects of deity: feminine and masculine, the Goddess and the God" (Weinstein, *Positive Magic,* 68).

"You were shown these things so that you might know that the LORD is God; besides him there is no other" (Deut. 4:35).

"Acknowledge and take to heart this day that the LORD is God in heaven above and on the earth below. There is no other" (Deut. 4:39).

"I am God, and there is no other; I am God, and there is none like me" (Isa. 46:9).

"For I am God, and not man—the Holy One among you" (Hos. 11:9b).

"They exchanged the truth of God for a lie, and worshiped and served created things rather than the Creator—who is forever praised. Amen" (Rom. 1:25).

"To the only God our Savior be glory, majesty, power and authority, through Jesus Christ our Lord, before all ages, now and forevermore! Amen" (Jude 25).

Jesus Christ

There are various views among neo-pagans regarding Jesus Christ. The following are a sample:

"I have heard of one witch who put a portrait of Jesus in her private sanctuary because, she said, he was a great white witch and knew the secret of the

"In the beginning was the Word, and the Word was with God, and the Word was God" (John 1:1; cf. vv. 14, 18).

"'I told you that you would die in your sins; if you do not believe that I am the one I claim to be, you will indeed die in your sins'" (John 8:24).

70

coven of thirteen" (Valiente, *ABC of Witchcraft,* 14).

"I believe he [Jesus] was a witch. He worked miracles or what we would call magic, cured people and did most things expected from a witch. He had his coven of thirteen" (Crowther and Crowther, *Secrets of Ancient Witchcraft,* 164).

"[We reject] the Christians' insistence that Jesus was God Incarnate; that the carpenter of Nazareth . . . was in fact the creator of the Cosmos. . . . we cannot find that he ever claimed to be God. The claim seems to us to have been imposed on him later, and to be a distortion of his actual message (with which any witch or occultist would agree) that divinity resides in all of us. If it shone through him more brightly than through most other people in history, that is another matter" (Farrar and Farrar, *Witches Bible Compleat,* 2:177).

"I [Jesus] am the way and the truth and the life. No one comes to the Father except through me" (John 14:6).

"Thomas said to him [Jesus], 'My Lord and my God!'" (John 20:28).

"Theirs are the patriarchs [the Jews], and from them is traced the human ancestry of Christ, who is God over all, forever praised! Amen" (Rom. 9:5).

"Your attitude should be the same as that of Christ Jesus: Who, being in very nature God, did not consider equality with God something to be grasped" (Phil. 2:5–6).

"Jesus said to them, 'I have shown you many great miracles from the Father. For which of these do you stone me?' 'We are not stoning you for any of these,' replied the Jews, 'but for blasphemy, because you, a mere man, claim to be god'" (John 10:32–33).

"To those who through the righteousness of our God and Savior Jesus Christ have received a faith as precious as ours" (2 Peter 1:1).

Humanity

"A spiritual path that is not stagnant ultimately leads one to the understanding of one's own divine nature. Thou art Goddess. Thou art God" (Adler, *Drawing Down the Moon,* ix).

"No matter how diverse Neo-Pagans' ideas about deities, almost all of them have some kind of 'Thou Art God/dess' concept" (Adler, *Drawing Down the Moon,* 202).

"So God created man in his own image, in the image of God he created him; male and female he created them" (Gen. 1:27).

"God is not a man, that he should lie, nor a son of man, that he should change his mind" (Num. 23:19).

"But the Egyptians are men and not God" (Isa. 31:3).

Sin

"We are aware of our own goodness and strength, and we are not afraid to admit it. We are not sinners and we know it" (Valerie Voigt, "Being a Pagan in a 9-to-5 World," 173).

"We have no concept of sin, no score card, in the way Christians understand. We have no concept of salvation, although it's certainly possible to do something wrong" (Paul Suliin, correspondence with author).

"'. . . for there is no one who does not sin'" (2 Chron. 6:36).

"Surely I was sinful at birth, sinful from the time my mother conceived me" (Ps. 51:5).

"All of us have become like one who is unclean, and all our righteous acts are like filthy rags" (Isa. 64:6).

"'There is no one righteous, not even one'" (Rom. 3:10).

"For all have sinned and fall short of the glory of God" (Rom. 3:23).

Reincarnation

"Most witches do believe in some form of reincarnation" (Starhawk, *Spiral Dance*, 84).

"Rebirth is not considered to be condemnation to an endless, dreary round of suffering, as in Eastern religions. Instead, it is seen as the great gift of the Goddess" (Starhawk, *Spiral Dance*, 27).

"Most Witches believe that human beings do not necessarily have immortal souls. The Craft promises 'rebirth among those you love' as the reward of the true initiates (the complete opposite of Eastern concepts)" (Kelly, *Neo-Pagan Witchcraft I*, introduction).

"There are two theories of how the circumstances of rebirth are determined. One is that the soul itself decides, based on what it feels it most needs to continue its advancement towards godhood" (Serith, *Pagan Family*, 198).

"But when the kindness and love of God our Savior appeared, he saved us, not because of righteous things we had done, but because of his mercy" (Titus 3:4–5).

"But now he has appeared once for all at the end of the ages to do away with sin by the sacrifice of himself. Just as man is destined to die once, and after that to face judgment, so Christ was sacrificed once to take away the sins of many people" (Heb. 9:26–28).

"The Lord knows how to rescue godly men from trials and to hold the unrighteous for the day of judgment, while continuing their punishment" (2 Peter 2:9).

"We are confident, I say, and would prefer to be away from the body and at home with the Lord" (2 Cor. 5:8).

Salvation

"We don't have a Devil to blame our mistakes on and we need no Savior to save us from a non-existent Hell" (Valerie Voigt, "Being a Pagan in a 9-to-5 World," 173).

"We can open new eyes and see that there is nothing to be saved *from*, no struggle of life *against* the universe, no God outside the world to be feared and obeyed" (Starhawk, *Spiral Dance*, 14).

"The kingdom of God is within you" (Adler, *Drawing Down the Moon*, 454).

"They [witches] feel that all should be free to choose the religion that best suits them. It would seem obvious that there can be no one religion for all" (Buckland, *Complete Book of Witchcraft*, 99).

"All religions lead in the same direction, simply taking different paths to get there" (Buckland, *Complete Book of Witchcraft*, 99).

"But when the kindness and love of God our Savior appeared, he saved us, not because of righteous things we had done, but because of his mercy" (Titus 3:4).

"For God so loved the world that he gave his one and only Son, that whoever believes in him shall not perish but have eternal life" (John 3:16).

"'I told you that you would die in your sins; if you do not believe that I am the one I claim to be, you will indeed die in your sins'" (John 8:24).

"Salvation is found in no one else, for there is no other name under heaven given to men by which we must be saved" (Acts 4:12).

"For the wages of sin is death, but the gift of God is eternal life in Christ Jesus our Lord" (Rom. 6:23).

"If you confess with your mouth, 'Jesus is Lord,' and believe in your heart that God raised him from the dead, you will be saved" (Rom. 10:9).

"For it is by grace you have been saved, through faith—and this not from yourselves, it is the gift of God—not by works, so that no one can boast" (Eph. 2:8–9).

Occultic Practices

"In Wicca it's [magic] given a more prominent place. . . . Wicca is a religion that embraces magic" (Cunningham, *Truth About Witchcraft*, 64–65).

"Wicca is magic" (Stewart Farrar, *What Witches Do*, 137).

"Magic . . . is an element common to all traditions of Witchcraft" and "Magic is the craft of Witchcraft" (Starhawk, *Spiral Dance*, 13, 109).

"Let no one be found among you . . . who practices divination or sorcery, interprets omens, engages in witchcraft, or casts spells, or who is a medium or spiritist or who consults the dead. Anyone who does these things is detestable to the LORD" (Deut. 18:10–12).

"I warn you, as I did before, that those who live like this [e.g., including those who practice witchcraft—v. 20] will not inherit the kingdom of God" (Gal. 5:21).

73

Occultic Practices (cont.)

"One of the objects of present-day witches' rites is to contact the spirits of those who have been witches in their past lives on earth" (Valiente, *ABC of Witchcraft*, 157).

"I always encourage children to have dreams . . . in which they will meet their spirit guides or animal helpers" (Cabot, in Cabot and Cowan, *Power of the Witch*, 278).

"Divination in all its forms has always been an important part of the witch's craft" (Valiente, *ABC of Witchcraft*, 117).

"Nor did they repent of their murders, their magic arts, their sexual immorality or their thefts" (Rev. 9:21).

"'But the cowardly, the unbelieving, the vile, the murderers, the sexually immoral, those who practice magic arts, the idolaters and all liars—their place will be in the fiery lake of burning sulfur. This is the second death'" (Rev. 21:8).

Sources

Margot Adler, *Drawing Down the Moon: Witches, Druids, Goddess-Worshippers, and Other Pagans in America Today*, rev. and expanded ed. (Boston: Beacon Press, 1986).

Raymond Buckland, *Buckland's Complete Book of Witchcraft* (St. Paul: Llewellyn, 1988).

Laurie Cabot and Tom Cowan, *Power of the Witch* (New York: Dell, 1989).

Arnold Crowther and Patricia Crowther, *The Secrets of Ancient Witchcraft with the Witches Tarot* (Secaucus, N.J.: University Books, 1974).

Scott Cunningham, *The Truth About Witchcraft Today* (St. Paul: Llewellyn, 1988).

Janet Farrar and Stewart Farrar, *A Witches Bible Compleat* (New York: Magickal Childe, 1984).

Stewart Farrar, *What Witches Do: The Modern Coven Revealed* (London: Sphere Books, 1973).

Prudence Jones and Caitlín Matthews, eds., *Voices from the Circle: The Heritage of Western Paganism* (Wellingborough, Northamptonshire, England: Aquarian Press, 1990).

Aidan Kelly, ed., *Cults and New Religions: Neo-Pagan Witchcraft I* (New York: Garland, 1990).

Ceisiwr Serith, *The Pagan Family: Handing the Old Ways Down* (St. Paul: Llewellyn, 1971).

Starhawk (Miriam Simos), *Dreaming the Dark: Magic, Sex and Politics*, new ed. (Boston: Beacon Press, 1988).

Starhawk (Miriam Simos), *The Spiral Dance: A Rebirth of the Ancient Religion of the Great Goddess* (San Francisco: Harper & Row, 1979).

Paul Suliin, correspondence with the author.

Doreen Valiente, *An ABC of Witchcraft: Past and Present* (New York: St. Martin's Press, 1973).

Valerie Voigt, "Being a Pagan in a 9-to-5 World," in *Witchcraft Today, Book One: The Modern Craft Movement*, ed. Chas S. Clifton (St. Paul: Llewellyn, 1992).

Marion Weinstein, *Positive Magic: Occult Self-Help*, rev. ed. (Custer, Wash.: Phoenix, 1981).

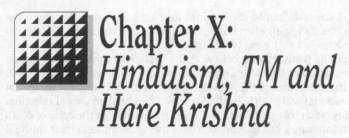# Chapter X:
Hinduism, TM and Hare Krishna

Author: J. Isamu Yamamoto; summary by Alan W. Gomes

Background

Hinduism is a major world religion most closely associated with India. To Indian Hindus, Hinduism is as much a culture and a way of life as it is a set of religious beliefs. The Aryans, who invaded India in the second millennium B.C., merged their religious views and practices with the indigenous people. These views were expressed in the form of religious hymns, which were eventually collected and written down to form the Vedas. (*Veda* means "knowledge" in Sanskrit.) The Vedas emphasized rituals to various gods. Through the rise of the Brahmin priestly class in the first millennium B.C., Brahma, Vishnu, and Siva became the main deities in the Indian pantheon. Other sacred texts were added besides the Vedas.

Other important developments include yoga in various forms, including bhakti, the devotion to a personal god. Bhakti is the most popular form of contemporary Hinduism, with most people worshiping either Siva or an avatar (i.e., incarnation) of Vishnu (such as Krisna or Rama). The Bhagavad-Gita and the Puranas are the writings that most fully treat these deities.

Hinduism took root in the United States in several forms. In nineteenth-century America, the writings of Emerson and Thoreau served as a conduit for aspects of Hindu philosophy. Later, a number of gurus came to the United States to spread Hindu teachings. However, the two main movements that drew particular attention to Hinduism in the United States were Transcendental Meditation (TM), led by the Maharishi Mahesh Yogi, and Hare Krishna (the International Society for Krishna Consciousness, or ISKCON), founded by the late Abhay Charan De Bhaktivedanta Swami Prabhupada. India has approximately 700 million Hindus, and there are more than one million Hindus in North America.

Summary of Beliefs

Hindus view **history** as eternally cyclical. The universe endures as long as the creator god Brahma lives; when he dies, the universe dissolves. Brahma is then born anew from a cosmic egg, beginning the cycle again. These cycles repeat endlessly. Each cycle can be divided into four ages. Currently we are in the fourth age (the Kali Age), when human corruption is at its height. All humanity will be destroyed at the end of this age.

Concerning **truth,** Hindus believe that all religions contain truth and no one religion can claim that its teachings on truth are absolute. At the same time, they hold that the Vedas are the highest expression of truth and that those who reject its teachings will go to hell. Hindus reject the Christian view of **salvation.** Instead, they teach that unenlightened souls move through the cycle of death and rebirth (*samsara*), but may break free of this cycle through their spiritual efforts and achieve the ultimate salvation of their souls, which is total absorption into Brahman.

Hindus believe that **Jesus Christ** was one of a number of great holy men, but was not perfect. They also reject as absurd the notion that Jesus suffered on the cross; as an enlightened holy man he was beyond pain and suffering. Concerning **God,** Hindus are polytheists. They believe that there are many gods who protect humankind. However, Brahman is the creator god and is regarded as the greatest. Yet Hindus are pantheistic, believing that true enlightenment consists in knowing that we are one with Brahman, that we are god. This realization is achieved through various spiritual practices, such as yoga.

Parallel Comparison Chart

Hinduism, TM and Hare Krishna	The Bible

History

"The four Ages known as Krta, Treta, Dvapara and Kali comprise 12,000 divine years [equal to about 4,320,000 human years during one cycle of these Ages]" (Markandeya Purana 43).	"In the beginning, O Lord, you laid the foundations of the earth, and the heavens are the work of your hands. They will perish.... But you remain the same, and your years will never end" (Heb. 1:10–12).
"In the Kali Age [present evil age], men will be afflicted by old age, disease, and hunger.... Then the Age will change, deluding their minds like a dream, by the force of fate, and when the Golden Age begins, those left over from the Kali Age will be the progenitors of the Golden Age.... Thus there is eternal continuity from Age to Age" (Linga Purana 1.40.72–83).	"Jesus Christ is the same yesterday and today and forever" (Heb. 13:8). "Then I saw a new heaven and a new earth, for the first heaven and the first earth passed away.... There will be no more death or mourning or crying or pain, for the old order of things has passed away" (Rev. 21:1, 4).

Absolute Truth

"Those sinners who have constantly condemned Vedas, gods or brahmins, those who have ignored the beneficial teachings of Purana and Itihasa . . . all these fall into these hells" (Vamana Purana 12.1).

"Hinduism has no fixed creed by which it may be said to stand or fall, for it is convinced that the spirit will outgrow the creed. For the Hindu every religion is true, if only its adherents sincerely and honestly follow it" (Radhakrishnan, *Religion and Society*, 53).

"Religion should not be confused with fixed intellectual conceptions, which are all mind-made. Any religion which claims finality and absoluteness desires to impose its own opinions on the rest of the world" (Radhakrishnan, *Religion and Society*, 52).

"Have nothing to do with godless myths" (1 Tim. 4:7).

"I am not ashamed of the gospel, because it is the power of God for the salvation of everyone who believes" (Rom. 1:16).

Jesus said, "I tell you the truth, until heaven and earth disappear, not the smallest letter, not the least stroke of a pen, will by any means disappear from the Law until everything is accomplished" (Matt. 5:18).

"Grace and truth came through Jesus Christ. No one has ever seen God, but God the One and Only, who is at the Father's side, has made him known" (John 1:17–18).

"I have not spoken in secret, from somewhere in a land of darkness; I have not said to Jacob's descendants, 'Seek me in vain.' I, the LORD, speak the truth; I declare what is right" (Isa. 45:19).

"Jesus answered, 'I am the way and the truth and the life. No one comes to the Father except through me'" (John 14:6).

Salvation of the Soul

"He who in fancy forms desires, because of his desires is born [again] here and there" (Mundaka Upanisad 3.2.2).

"The early Christian church accepted the doctrine of reincarnation. . . . The truth is that man reincarnates on earth until he has consciously regained his status as a son of God" (Yogananda, *Autobiography of a Yogi*, 199).

"When the dweller in the body has overcome the gunas [essence of nature] that cause this body, then he is made free

"As [Jesus] went along, he saw a man blind from birth. His disciples asked him, 'Rabbi, who sinned, this man or his parents, that he was born blind?' 'Neither this man nor his parents,' said Jesus" (John 9:1–3).

"Just as man is destined to die once, and after that to face judgment, so Christ was sacrificed once to take away the sins of many people" (Heb. 9:27–28).

Jesus said, "For my Father's will is that everyone who looks to the Son and believes in him shall have eternal life, and

Salvation of the Soul (cont.)

from birth and death, from pain and decay: He becomes immortal" (Bhagavad-Gita 14.20).

I will raise him up at the last day" (John 6:40).

"There can be no real perfection for us except by our inner self" (Aurobindo, *The Life Divine*, 931).

"By one sacrifice [Christ] has made perfect forever those who are being made holy" (Heb. 10:14).

"When a Yogin pronounces the syllable OM, it reaches the crown of his head. When a Yogin is absorbed in the syllable OM, he becomes eternal. . . . He becomes one with Brahman. . . . He wins absorption in Brahman, in the supreme ultimate Self" (Markandeya Purana 39.6, 16).

Jesus said, "For God so loved the world that he gave his one and only Son, that whoever believes in him shall not perish but have eternal life. . . . Whoever believes in the Son has eternal life, but whoever rejects the Son will not see life, for God's wrath remains on him" (John 3:16, 36).

Jesus Christ

"I don't think Christ ever suffered or Christ could suffer. . . . It's a pity that Christ is talked of in terms of suffering" (Yogi, *Meditations of Maharishi Mahesh Yogi*, 123–24).

"[Jesus] said to them, 'How foolish you are, and how slow of heart to believe all that the prophets have spoken! Did not the Christ have to suffer these things and then enter his glory?'" (Luke 24:25–26).

"No man on earth has ever maintained spiritual poise all through his life. The Jesus who declared that men must not resist evil if they are to become the sons of the Father who makes his sun shine upon good men and bad, and his rain to fall upon the just and the unjust, was the same Jesus who cursed the fig-tree and drove the tradesmen from the temple" (Radhakrishnan, *A Sourcebook in Indian Philosophy*, 634).

"Therefore, since we have a great high priest who has gone through the heavens, Jesus the Son of God, let us hold firmly to the faith we profess. For we do not have a high priest who is unable to sympathize with our weaknesses, but we have one who has been tempted in every way, just as we are—yet was without sin" (Heb. 4:14–15).

"[Christ] committed no sin, and no deceit was found in his mouth" (1 Peter 2:22).

"But you know that [Christ] appeared so that he might take away our sins. And in him is no sin" (1 John 3:5).

"The great masters of India mold their lives by the same godly ideals that animated Jesus. . . . Freemen all, lords of themselves, the Yogi-Christs of India are part of the immortal fraternity" (Yo-

Jesus warned, "Watch out that no one deceives you. For many will come in my name, claiming, 'I am the Christ,' and will deceive many" (Matt. 24:4–5).

gananda, *Autobiography of a Yogi*, 195–96).

"Whoso in Man knows Brahman, knows the highest Lord. . . . Whereas the gods who Brahman know revere Brahman as the highest, best" (Atharva Veda 10.7.17, 24).

"Therefore God exalted him to the highest place and gave him the name that is above every name, that at the name of Jesus every knee should bow, in heaven and on earth and under the earth, and every tongue confess that Jesus Christ is Lord, to the glory of God the Father" (Phil. 2:9–11).

God

"That the gods ever may be with us for our gain, our guardians day by day unceasing in their care. May the auspicious favour of the gods be ours, on us descend the bounty of the righteous gods. The friendship of the gods have we devoutly sought; so may the gods extend our life that we may live" (Rg Veda 1.89.1–2).

"In the beginning this [universe] was Brahman alone. . . . So, whoever reveres any other deity, thinking: 'He is one, and I am another,' does not [rightly] understand" (Brhadaranyaka Upanisad 1.4.10).

Lord Krisna declared, "Know that all beings have their birth in this. I am the origin of all this world and its dissolution as well. There is nothing whatever that is higher than I. . . . I am the syllable Aum [OM] in all the Vedas. . . . I am not in them [all beings]; they are in Me" (Bhagavad-Gita 7.6–8, 12).

"They become the ocean itself. . . . Whatever they are in this world, whether tiger, or lion, or wolf, or boar, or worm, or fly, or gnat, or mosquito, that they become. That which is the finest essence—this whole world has that as its self. That is Reality. That is *Atman*. That art thou, Svetaketu" (Chandogya Upanisad 6.10.1–3).

"Acknowledge and take to heart this day that the LORD is God in heaven above and on the earth below. There is no other" (Deut. 4:39).

"'You are my witnesses,' declares the LORD, 'and my servant whom I have chosen, so that you may know and believe me and understand that I am he. Before me no god was formed, nor will there be one after me'" (Isa. 43:10).

"In the beginning God created the heavens and the earth" (Gen. 1:1).

The God of Israel said, "I am the LORD, and there is no other; apart from me there is no God. . . . It is I who made the earth and created mankind upon it. . . . And there is no God apart from me, a righteous God and a Savior; there is none but me. . . . I am God, and there is no other; I am God, and there is none like me" (Isa. 45:5, 12, 21; 46:9).

"God said to Moses, 'I AM WHO I AM. This is what you are to say to the Israelites, "I AM has sent me"'" (Ex. 3:14).

"Hear, O Israel: The LORD our God, the LORD is one" (Deut. 6:4).

"'The most important [commandment],' answered Jesus, 'is this: "Hear, O Israel, the Lord our God, the Lord is one"'" (Mark 12:29).

God (cont.)

"He who finds his happiness within, his joy within, and likewise his light only within, that yogin becomes divine" (Bhagavad-Gita 5.24).

Sources

Sri Aurobindo, *The Life Divine* (New York: Greystone Press, 1949).

Bhagavad-Gita: Sacred texts that together with the Puranas, the Sutras, and other texts constitute the writing known as *Smrtis*.

Markandeya Purana, Linga Purana, Vamana Purana: Sacred texts in the Puranas that together with Bhagavad-Gita, the Sutras, and other texts constitute the writings known as *Smrtis*.

Sarvepalli Radhakrishnan, *Religion and Society* (London: George Allen & Unwin, 1959).

Mundaka Upanisad, Brhadaranyaka Upanisad, Chandogya Upanisad: Sacred texts in the Upanisads that together with the Vedas constitute the writings known as *Sruti*.

Atharva Veda, Rg Veda: Sacred texts in the Vedas that together with the Upanisads constitute the writings known as *Sruti*.

Paramahansa Yogananda, *Autobiography of a Yogi* (Los Angeles: Self-Realization Fellowship, 1972).

Maharishi Mahesh Yogi, *Meditations of Maharishi Mahesh Yogi* (New York: Bantam, 1968).

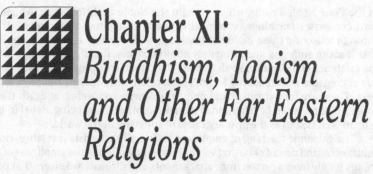

Chapter XI:
Buddhism, Taoism and Other Far Eastern Religions

Author: J. Isamu Yamamoto; summary by Alan W. Gomes

Background

Prominent among many Far Eastern movements are Buddhism, Taoism, Confucianism, Bon, and Shinto. **Buddhism** was founded by Siddhartha Gautama (560 B.C.). While meditating in front of a fig tree, Gautama achieved enlightenment (*Buddha* means "enlightened one") and discovered the Four Noble Truths. After Buddha's passing, several different Buddhist schools or traditions formed, each interpreting his *dharma* (i.e., Buddha's doctrine) differently. The two major Buddhist branches are Theravada ("the doctrine of the elders") and Mahayana ("the great wheel"), the Mahayana branch being further subdivided into many subgroupings or schools.

Taoism emerged in China around the sixth or seventh century B.C. Tao, which means "the way," is variously interpreted. Taoism has evolved into philosophical and religious Taoism. Philosophical Taoism is rational and contemplative, while religious Taoism draws on magic and the occult to attain physical immortality. **Confucius** (551–449 B.C.), born in Shantung, China, sought to reform the corrupt political system of his day. He advanced a system of ethics that is still influential in the lives of many Chinese. **Bon** is a shamanistic religion found primarily in Tibet. Bon is animistic, believing in spirit beings behind the various forces of nature. Bon shamans use their powers to control these spirit beings as well as to effect physical healing.

Shinto, which means "way of the gods," originated in Japan. Adherents of Shinto worshiped Amaterasu Omikami, the Sun Goddess, at the imperial shrine until 1945. Shintoists believe that all Japanese emperors are descendants of this Sun Goddess. Shintoists also build shrines to the *kami* (local deities) and through magical formulas and incantations hope to gain their assistance in warding off evil.

Summary of Beliefs

Concerning **human suffering,** Buddhists believe that all human life is grievous. Suffering is caused by ignorance and the desires of the senses. This is outlined in the Four Noble Truths, which contain the Noble Eightfold Path, which in turn comprises teachings on ethical conduct, discipline, and wisdom. It is through following these Buddhist teachings that one may escape the craving that leads to suffering and ultimately attain nirvana. Buddhists strongly deny the existence of the **human soul;** instead, they teach that people are made up of five aggregates: material form, feeling, perception, dispositions, and consciousness. These are impermanent and only temporarily connected; at death these constituent parts can be refashioned to make another living being. Belief in the human soul is seen as the primary cause of suffering in the world.

The Buddhist teaching of **emptiness** is that all that exists is relative, nonsubstantial, and devoid of lasting value. True recognition of the emptiness of all things totally frees a person from attachments and ultimately delivers that person from suffering. Buddhist conceptions of **salvation** vary among the different schools: renunciation of the world (Theravada), meditation (Zen), faith in the compassion of Amida Buddha (Amida Buddhism), chanting incantations from the Lotus Sutra (Nichiren), and various esoteric spiritual techniques (Tibetan). In Taoism one must seek harmony with the world through passivity in order to realize salvation, while in Confucianism salvation is attained through following the ethical conduct taught by Confucius.

Concerning **God,** some Buddhist traditions discourage any speculations about a deity (Theravada, Zen), while others invoke deities as part of their spiritual exercises (Tibetan). The Taoist tradition defines the Tao as the Absolute, but not as a supreme being. Likewise, Confucius deliberately avoided in his teachings any talk about heavenly beings.

Parallel Comparison Chart

Buddhism, Taoism ...	The Bible
Human Suffering	
"This is the noble truth of sorrow. Birth is sorrow, age is sorrow, disease is sorrow, death is sorrow.... in short, all the five components of individuality is sorrow" (*Samyutta-nikaya* 5:4; from the Pali Canon).	Jesus said, "You will grieve, but your grief will turn to joy.... Now is your time of grief, but I will see you again and you will rejoice, and no one will take away your joy" (John 16:20, 22).
"To one who is thus not wisely reflecting, one of six speculative views may arise as though it were real and true: 'there is self for me.' ... fettered by this fetter, the ordinary uninstructed person is not freed from birth, from aging and	Jesus then said, "I have told you these things, so that in me you may have peace. In this world you will have trouble. But take heart! I have overcome the world" (John 16:33).

dying or from grief, sorrow, suffering, lamentation and despair. I say that he is not freed from suffering" (*Majjhima-Nikaya* I, 8).

"While realizing that there is no permanent or immutable entity called the 'self,' [the Buddha] also found that belief in such an entity led to further suffering. Belief in a permanent entity such as the *atman* often led to selfishness and egoism. This, for him, was the root cause of craving and its attendant suffering" (David J. Kalupahana, *Buddhist Philosophy*, 38).

"Dear friends, do not be surprised at the painful trial you are suffering, as though something strange were happening to you. But rejoice that you participate in the sufferings of Christ, so that you may be overjoyed when his glory is revealed. If you are insulted because of the name of Christ, you are blessed, for the Spirit of glory and of God rests on you. If you suffer, it should not be as a murderer or thief or any other kind of criminal, or even as a meddler. However, if you suffer as a Christian, do not be ashamed, but praise God that you bear that name" (1 Peter 4:12–16).

The Human Soul

"Persons are a conglomeration of skandhas, elements and sense-fields, devoid of a self or anything belonging to a self. Consciousness arises from ignorance, karma and craving, and it keeps going by settling down in the grasping at form" (*Lanleavatara Sutra*, 68).

"Buddhism stands unique in the history of human thought in denying the existence of such a Soul, Self, or *Atman*. According to the teaching of the Buddha, the idea of self is an imaginary, false belief which has no corresponding reality, and it produces harmful thoughts of 'me' and 'mine,' selfish desire, craving, attachment, hatred, ill-will, conceit, pride, egoism, and other defilements, impurities, and problems" (Walpola Rahula, *What the Buddha Taught*, 51).

The Buddha taught, "I had no notion of a self, or of a being, or of a soul, or of a

"As the deer pants for streams of water, so my soul pants for you, O God. My soul thirsts for God, for the living God" (Ps. 42:1–2).

"Find rest, O my soul, in God alone" (Ps. 62:5).

"The LORD is my shepherd, I shall lack nothing. . . . he restores my soul" (Ps. 23:1, 3).

"But the things that come out of the mouth come from the heart, and these make a man 'unclean.' For out of the heart come evil thoughts, murder, adultery, sexual immorality, theft, false testimony, slander" (Matt. 15:18–19).

"Hear, O Israel: The LORD our God, the LORD is one. Love the LORD your God with all your heart and with all your soul and with all your strength" (Deut. 6:4–5).

"Jesus replied: ' "Love the Lord your God with all your heart and with all

The Human Soul (cont.)

person, nor had I any notion or non-notion" (*Vajracchedika*, 14).

"Nirvana is definitely no annihilation of self, because there is no self to annihilate. . . . An Arahant [Buddhist saint] after his death is often compared to a fire gone out when the supply of wood is over, or to the flame of a lamp gone out when the wick and oil are finished. Here it should be clearly and distinctly understood, without any confusion, that what is compared to a flame or a fire gone out is *not* Nirvana, but the 'being' composed of the Five Aggregates who realized Nirvana" (Walpola Rahula, *What the Buddha Taught*, 37, 41–42).

your soul and with all your mind." This is the first and greatest commandment'" (Matt. 22:37–38).

"Keep yourselves in God's love as you wait for the mercy of our Lord Jesus Christ to bring you to eternal life" (Jude 21).

"The gift of God is eternal life in Christ Jesus our Lord" (Rom. 6:23).

Jesus said, "My sheep listen to my voice; I know them, and they follow me. I give them eternal life, and they shall never perish" (John 10:27–28a).

"God has given us eternal life, and this life is in his Son" (1 John 5:11).

Emptiness

"Impermanent and unstable are all conditioned things" (*Lalitavistara*. XIII, 95).

"So one who is convinced of the emptiness of everything has no likes or dislikes. For he knows that that which he might like is just empty, and he sees it as just empty" (*Sikshasamuccaya, 264*).

"Regard the world as void" (*Suttanipata*, 119).

Jesus Christ is the same yesterday and today and forever" (Heb. 13:8).

The Lord says, "so is my word that goes out from my mouth: It will not return to me empty, but will accomplish what I desire and achieve the purpose for which I sent it" (Isa. 55:11).

Jesus Christ "who descended is the very one who ascended higher than all the heavens, in order to fill the whole universe" (Eph. 4:10).

Salvation

"Be lamps unto yourselves. Be a refuge unto yourselves. Do not turn to any external refuge. . . . Work out your own salvation with diligence" (*Mahaparinibbana-sutta* 2:33; 6:10; from the Pali Canon).

"For it is by grace you have been saved, through faith—and this not from yourselves, it is the gift of God—not by works, so that no one can boast" (Eph. 2:8–9).

"A Bodhisattva resolves: I take upon myself the burden of all suffering" (*Sikshasamuccaya,* 280 [Mahayana Buddhism]).

"Amitabha, the Protector ... endowed with great compassion, created for the world's saving" (*Aryatarabhattarikanamashtottarasatakastotra,* 12–13 [Amida Buddhism]).

"And when you're in the company of your master, do not look for faults and virtues, good and bad. If you do, you'll see him as a mass of faults. Just practise clarity of mind and exert yourselves" (Milarepa, *mGur-h Bum* [Tibetan Buddhism]).

"What you do not want done to yourself, do not do to others" (Confucius, *Analects,* 15:23).

"Surely [Jesus Christ] took up our infirmities and carried our sorrows. . . . he was crushed for our iniquities; the punishment that brought us peace was upon him, and by his wounds we are healed. We all, like sheep, have gone astray, each of us has turned to his own way; and the LORD has laid on him the iniquity of us all" (Isa. 53:4–6).

"We have one who speaks to the Father in our defense—Jesus Christ, the Righteous One. He is the atoning sacrifice for our sins, and not only for ours but also for the sins of the whole world" (1 John 2:1–2).

"Because Jesus lives forever, he has a permanent priesthood. Therefore he is able to save completely those who come to God through him, because he always lives to intercede for them. Such a high priest meets our need—one who is holy, blameless, pure, set apart from sinners, exalted above the heavens" (Heb. 7:24–26).

"Dear friends, do not believe every spirit, but test the spirits to see whether they are from God, because many false prophets have gone out into the world. This is how you can recognize the Spirit of God: Every spirit that acknowledges that Jesus Christ has come in the flesh is from God, but every spirit that does not acknowledge Jesus is not from God" (1 John 4:1–3).

"See to it that no one takes you captive through hollow and deceptive philosophy, which depends on human tradition and the basic principles of this world rather than on Christ. For in Christ all the fullness of the Deity lives in bodily form" (Col. 2:8–9).

Jesus said, "In everything, do to others what you would have them do to you" (Matt. 7:12; see also Luke 6:31).

God

"Yet you [the Buddha] preach compassion for all beings, O you God above the Gods! . . . Let us therefore worship you, the chief and best of men, worthy of our worship" (*Sikshasamuccaya,* 259 [Mahayana Buddhism]).

"To go to him [the Buddha] for refuge, to praise and to honour him, to abide in his religion, that is fit for those with sense. The only Protector, he is without faults or their residues; the All-knowing, he has all the virtues, and that without fail" (*Matrceta, Satapancasatkastotra,* I, 2–3).

"By the enjoyment of all desires, to which one devotes oneself just as one pleases, it is by such practice as this that one may speedily gain Buddhahood. With the enjoyment of all desires, to which one devotes oneself just as one pleases, in union with one's chosen divinity, one worships oneself, the Supreme One" (*Guhyasamajatantra,* ch. 7 [Tibetan Buddhism]).

"And God spoke all these words: 'I am the LORD your God. . . . You shall have no other gods before me. . . . You shall not bow down to them or worship them; for I, the LORD your God, am a jealous God" (Ex. 20:1–3, 5).

"The LORD is gracious and righteous; our God is full of compassion" (Ps. 116:5).

"Therefore God exalted him to the highest place and gave him the name that is above every name, that at the name of Jesus every knee should bow, in heaven and on earth and under the earth, and every tongue confess that Jesus Christ is Lord, to the glory of God the Father" (Phil. 2:9–11).

"The eternal God is your refuge" (Deut. 33:27).

God says about his Son Jesus Christ, "You have loved righteousness and hated wickedness; therefore God, your God, has set you above your companions" (Heb. 1:9).

In addition, the apostle Peter called Jesus, "the Holy and Righteous One" (Acts 3:14).

"The wrath of God is being revealed from heaven against all the godlessness and wickedness of men who suppress the truth by their wickedness, since what may be known about God is plain to them, because God has made it plain to them. For since the creation of the world God's invisible qualities—his eternal power and divine nature—have been clearly seen, being understood from what has been made, so that men are without excuse.

"For although they knew God, they neither glorified him as God nor gave thanks to him, but their thinking became futile and their foolish hearts were darkened. Although they claimed

86

to be wise, they became fools and exchanged the glory of the immortal God for images made to look like mortal man and birds and animals and reptiles.

"Therefore God gave them over in the sinful desires of their hearts to sexual impurity for the degrading of their bodies with one another. They exchanged the truth of God for a lie, and worshiped and served created things rather than the Creator—who is forever praised. Amen" (Rom. 1:18–25).

"For whoever exalts himself will be humbled" (Matt. 23:12; Luke 14:11; 18:14).

"The Nameless is the origin of Heaven and Earth" (*The Way of Lao-tzu,* 1).

God told Moses to tell the Israelites that his name is "I am who I am. . . . This is my name forever, the name by which I am to be remembered from generation to generation" (Ex. 3:14–15).

"In the beginning God created the heavens and the earth" (Gen. 1:1).

"All things in the world come from being. And being comes from non-being" (*The Way of Lao-tzu,* 40).

"Through him [Jesus] all things were made; without him nothing was made that has been made" (John 1:3).

Sources

Aryatarabhattarikanamashtottarasatakastotra, 12–13 (Amida Buddhism).
Confucius, *Analects,* 15:23.
Guhyasamajatantra, ch. 7 (Tibetan Buddhism).
David J. Kalupahana, *Buddhist Philosophy: A Historical Analysis* (Honolulu: University Press of Hawaii, 1976).
Lalitavistara, XIII, 95.
Lanleavatara Sutra, 68.
Mahaparinibbana-sutta 2:33; 6:10; from the Pali Canon.
Majjhima-Nikaya I, 8.
Matrceta, Satapancasatkastotra, I, 2–3.
Milarepa, mGur-h Bum (Tibetan Buddhism).
Walpola Rahula, *What the Buddha Taught* (New York: Grove Press, 1974).
Samyutta-nikaya 5:4; from the Pali Canon.
Sikshasamuccaya, 280 (Mahayana Buddhism).
Suttanipata, 119.
Vajracchedika, 14.
The Way of Lao-tzu, 1.

Chapter XII:
Satanism

Authors: Robert and Gretchen Passantino; summary by Alan W. Gomes

Background

The term *satanism* is applied to those systems of belief that entail the worship of "Satan"—however Satan is defined. This latter point is crucial, because few "mainstream" Satanists (such as the late Anton LaVey) believe in the existence of a personal Devil (such as the Bible teaches). Rather, the overarching philosophy for most Satanists is hedonism: They seek self-indulgence and gratification. Many satanists see themselves as Satan, and their worship of "Satan" (themselves) consists in their self-indulgent lifestyle. The designation *Satan* is used because satanists see Christianity as their arch nemesis. Since "Satan" is the antithesis to and enemy of the Christian God, satanists "worship Satan" (i.e., indulge themselves) because they, too, unalterably oppose the Christian God. As LaVey, founder of the Church of Satan, said, "We don't worship Satan, we worship ourselves using the metaphorical representation of the qualities of Satan."

There are, however, some who do believe in a personal Devil and have given their allegiance to him. These are primarily "self-styled" (often teenage) Satanists—that is, those who invent their own system rather than aligning themselves with a group such as LaVey's.

Precise statistics on the number of satanic groups and practicing satanists are impossible to obtain, but rough estimates place the total number of self-professed satanists at less than 6,000 worldwide. Most are of the self-styled variety, practicing their own system either alone or in small groups. However, these small groups typically do not last long; those who continue tend to join one of the larger satanic churches, such as LaVey's. It is evident that, contrary to sensationalistic claims, there is no widespread satanic conspiracy. Also, although satanism is commonly confused with witchcraft, it is an entirely different belief system. (See "Goddess Worship, Witchcraft and Neo-paganism" above.)

Summary of Beliefs

(Because satanism is so varied and individualistic, the following summary should not be understood as speaking for all satanists. Rather, it is a summary of some beliefs held by certain well-known satanists.) Concerning the **Bible,** satanists reject its authority. Since they generally do not believe in God's existence, it follows that the Bible cannot be inspired by God. Nor do they regard their own Satanic Bible as inspired. Being antiauthoritarian, satanists reject obedience to any external standard.

There is a wide range of satanic views about **God.** As noted previously, most satanists do not believe in the existence of God at all. Those who do generally define "God" as a naturalistic force that can be harnessed for the satanist's own use. Some satanists deny that **Jesus Christ** even existed. In any case, the Jesus described in the Bible is despised as weak and ineffectual; he is the opposite of what satanists aspire to be. Satanists reject the reality of **sin** and consequently see no need for **salvation.** Instead, they believe that self-fulfillment is accomplished only through self-effort.

Parallel Comparison Chart

Note: Satanist beliefs are summarized in each instance rather than directly quoted for three reasons: (1) Satanists do not hold anyone's pronouncements as authoritative or binding on all satanists; (2) satanists are not uniform in their beliefs; and (3) satanists by and large ignore most distinctions in biblical theology because of their disdain for the Bible. However, each summary is representative of a significant number of satanists.

Satanists Believe	The Bible Teaches
The Bible	
Satanists reject the inspiration and authority of the Bible. Moreover, they do not consider their own writings, such as Anton LaVey's *Satanic Bible,* to be "revelation" or "inspired" or "divine."	Hebrews 4:12 warns, "The word of God is living and active. Sharper than any double-edged sword, it penetrates even to dividing soul and spirit, joints and marrow; it judges the thoughts and attitudes of the heart."
	Second Timothy 3:15–17 describes God's Word as "able to make you wise for salvation through faith in Christ Jesus" and "God-breathed and . . . useful for teaching, rebuking, correcting and training in righteousness, so that the man of God may be thoroughly equipped for every good work."

God

Most satanists reject belief in any supreme being or god, although some believe in a neutral, natural, nonmaterial universal force that they can use for their own power. A few believe in but reject the authority of the God of the Bible.

Romans 1:18–20 declares that all people know that God exists: "The wrath of God is being revealed from heaven against all the godlessness and wickedness of men who suppress the truth by their wickedness, since what may be known about God is plain to them, because God has made it plain to them. For since the creation of the world God's invisible qualities—his eternal power and divine nature—have been clearly seen, being understood from what has been made, so that men are without excuse."

Jesus Christ

Most satanists do not believe that Jesus Christ is a historical figure, much less that he is God incarnate or our savior. Those who admit to his historical existence view him as a weakling and a failure.

Peter affirmed the historicity of Jesus Christ: "We did not follow cleverly invented stories when we told you about the power and coming of our Lord Jesus Christ, but we were eyewitnesses of his majesty" (2 Peter 1:16; see also Luke 1:1–4; Acts 26:25–26). Jesus' power, wisdom, and courage were displayed in his willing self-sacrifice on our behalf, as when he declared, "I lay down my life for the sheep [sinners]. . . . The reason my Father loves me is that I lay down my life—only to take it up again. No one takes it from me, but I lay it down of my own accord. I have authority to lay it down and authority to take it up again" (John 10:15, 17–18).

Satan

Satanists worship Satan, whether they ascribe the title to themselves (most common), to some nonmaterial force they use for their own self-gratification (also popular), or to the evil spirit described in the Bible (a few, especially young satanists who grew up in Christian homes).

The Bible describes Satan as the chief fallen angel (Luke 10:18), Beelzebul (Matt. 10:25), "the evil one" (Matt. 5:37). Jesus' coming (and death—Col. 2:15) destroyed Satan's power: "I saw Satan fall like lightning from heaven" (Luke 10:18). Satan is called the original liar (John 8:44) and the one who accuses the righteous (Job 1:6–12; Rev. 12:10). He is also referred to as a ruler of this wicked world and evil spiritual forces (Eph. 2:2; 6:12; John 14:30). The ultimate destination of Satan and his demons is the lake of fire (Matt. 25:41; Rev. 20:10).

Human Beings

Satanists reject the idea that humans are accountable to God, society, or any standard of morals or ethics. Most satanists believe that the majority of humans are ignorant and deserve to be exploited by the satanist elite who are governed by rational self-interest.

Humanity was created perfect, sinless, and in God's image: "So God created man in his own image, in the image of God he created him; male and female he created them. God blessed them . . ." (Gen. 1:27–28a). Hebrews 2:14–18 describes the nature of humanity in terms of the perfect humanity of Christ in his incarnation and in contrast to humanity corrupted by sin: "Since the children have flesh and blood, he too shared in their humanity so that by his death he might destroy him who holds the power of death—that is, the devil—and free those who all their lives were held in slavery by their fear of death. For surely it is not angels he helps, but Abraham's descendants. For this reason he had to be made like his brothers in every way, in order that he might become a merciful and faithful high priest in service to God, and that he might make atonement for the sins of the people. Because he himself suffered when he was tempted, he is able to help those who are being tempted."

Sin and Salvation

Satanists reject the reality of sin, see no need for salvation, and believe self-fulfillment is accomplished wholly through self-effort.

By Adam and Eve's initial sin, humanity was condemned and made sinful (Rom. 5:12–21). "All have sinned and fall short of the glory of God" (Rom. 3:23), but humanity is not left without redemption, "and are justified freely by his grace through the redemption that came by Christ Jesus" (Rom. 3:24). Jesus Christ is the only way of salvation (Acts 4:12), and he promises, "I am the resurrection and the life. He who believes in me will live, even though he dies; and whoever lives and believes in me will never die" (John 11:25). Those who deny the reality of sin and think that they can be fulfilled through self-effort are condemned: "Woe to those who call evil good and good evil; who put darkness for light and light for darkness; who put bitter for sweet and sweet for bitter! Woe to those who are wise in their own eyes and clever in their own sight." (Isa. 5:20–21). Such people God will send to eternal punishment, but those who are saved by Jesus Christ receive eternal life (Matt. 25:46).

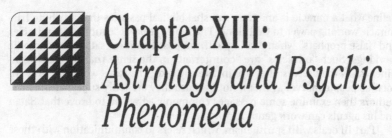

Chapter XIII:
Astrology and Psychic Phenomena

Authors: André Kole and Terry Holley; summary by Alan W. Gomes

(Note: Because this book is not about a particular cult but is an introduction to psychic phenomena in general, it does not follow the typical divisions of the other books and does not contain a parallel comparison chart. What follows instead is an overview of the book.)

Part I, "Introduction," begins with a definition and description of psychic powers. Categories of psychic powers include extrasensory perception (ESP, including telepathy, clairvoyance, precognition) and psychokinesis (i.e., "mind over matter," or the mind influencing external physical objects). The authors then consider the case made by those who advocate the existence of psychic powers. Such "evidence" includes testimonies of those who claim to have seen or exhibited such powers, including evidence from laboratory-controlled experiments. Various theories have been offered by believers in psychic phenomena to account for these alleged occurrences. Some theories include the notion that they are God-given gifts, that they are of demonic origin, and that they result from scientific principles not yet fully understood. In contrast, the authors conclude that it appears extremely unlikely that such powers exist. They argue that there are other, non-psychic explanations for such "evidence." (Specific cases are dealt with later.) The authors then explore why people believe in the existence of psychic phenomena in spite of the lack of solid evidence to support them. Reasons include deception; exaggeration; uncritical acceptance of what we are told; thinking that "seeing is believing," when in fact stage magicians and illusionists can make "normal" events appear to be supernatural; faulty reasoning; and basing beliefs solely on personal experience. The authors conclude the introduction with a discussion of principles for evaluating psychic claims, including the foundational importance of what Scripture says about evaluating truth claims; burden of proof issues; and the need of be cognizant of the various methods of trickery and deception.

Part II treats what the Bible has to say about psychic phenomena. The authors first consider the errant teaching of various popular Christian authors. Such authors wrongly conclude that the Bible teaches the reality of psychic powers, some affirming that Satan can work miracles. In contrast, the Bible teaches the limits of the power of Satan and demons and shows that they cannot perform miracles or energize anyone else to do so. The book's authors first define what a miracle is and then marshal biblical passages that attribute true miracle working power to God alone. The Bible speaks of "counterfeit" miracles and "false prophets" when dealing with supposed and real satanic or demonic workings. Such "miracles" are "counterfeit" in the sense that they lack genuineness in themselves; they are inherently fake. They are "wonders" only insofar as people marvel at them, not because they are truly supernatural. The authors then examine some passages commonly advanced to prove that Satan and his agents can work genuine miracles.

Part III deals with spiritualism, which refers to communication with those who live in the spirit world, often (though not always) departed human beings. The authors provide a brief history of spiritualist claims, including those of Swedenborg, the Fox sisters, and New Age channeling. A refutation of spiritualism follows, including a discussion of the biblical prohibitions against it and the exposés and confessions of famous spiritualists. The authors also examine and refute the various paranormal and normal sources of spiritualism.

Part IV treats parapsychology and psychics. The authors provide a history of parapsychological research, describe the alleged psychic abilities, and analyze the claims of famous psychics, including Uri Geller, Ted Serios, Sai Baba, and various "psychic detectives"—i.e., people who use their supposed psychic abilities to help police solve crimes. The authors investigate some of the more famous parapsychological experiments, demonstrating many fatal flaws with their methodology and controls. They scrutinize the claims of these famous psychics and reject them in light of a more detailed consideration of the facts.

Part V discusses fortune-telling in various forms, including astrology, tarot cards, crystal gazing, palmistry, Ouija boards, and numerology. The authors devote considerable attention to astrology, discussing its history, the number of modern-day practitioners, and various astrological practices and techniques. They present biblical passages condemning astrology and expose astrology's scientific and logical flaws. Likewise, the authors evaluate the claims of famous fortune tellers—including Nostradamus, Edgar Cayce, Jeane Dixon, and the increasingly popular "psychic phone networks"—and find them wanting.

The book concludes with tips for witnessing to those involved in psychic practices.

 # Chapter XIV:
Unmasking the Cults

Author: Alan W. Gomes; summary by Alan W. Gomes

(Note: Because this book is not about a particular cult but is an introduction to cults in general, it does not follow the typical divisions of the other books or contain a parallel comparison chart. What follows instead is an overview of the book.)

Part I attempts to answer a difficult and controversial yet foundational question: What is a cult? Cults generally have been defined in one of two ways: theologically and sociologically. Theological definitions focus on the group's belief system, specifically its deviation from Christian orthodoxy. Sociological definitions focus on behavioral characteristics of the group and its leaders. The theological definition is to be preferred, though the behavioral characteristics of cults must also be given due weight. The following definition of a cult is adopted: "A cult of Christianity is a group of people claiming to be Christian, who embrace a particular doctrinal system taught by an individual leader, group of leaders, or organization, which (system) denies (either explicitly or implicitly) one or more of the central doctrines of the Christian faith as taught in the sixty-six books of the Bible."

Part II provides statistics of how many people are involved in cults. This is difficult to answer, one reason being that definitions of what constitutes a cult vary so widely. Using the theological definition set forth in the book and considering only the two largest cults—Jehovah's Witnesses and the Mormon Church—there are more than 13 million cultists. Factoring in some of the smaller groups that also fit the definition, there are certainly at least 16 million cult adherents worldwide.

Part III offers an overview of theological characteristics commonly found in cults. Theological characteristics have to do with how the groups handle questions of religious doctrine. Some of the common theological characteristics include denial of the Trinity, denial of salvation by grace, devaluation of Christ's work, denial of the bodily resurrection, reduction of Scripture's absolute authority, redefinition of biblical terms, rejection of hell, emphasis on experience over doctrine, fixation with the end times, and faulty principles of biblical interpretation.

Part IV addresses the sociological characteristics of cults. The proper place and the limitations of the social sciences are examined. Considerable discussion is given to the question of brainwashing or mind control in cults. Those who advocate the mind-control model believe that some if not many cults employ unethical techniques of manipulation in which the "victims" (cult members) lose their ability to think autonomously. Thus mentally enslaved, the members are unable to evaluate involvement in the group and are highly unlikely to leave without outside intervention. Consequently, some who advocate the mind-control model also justify "deprogramming," a process that may involve abducting cult members and leading them, through a variety of confrontational techniques, to "snap out" of their mind-controlled state.

The mind-control thesis is to be thoroughly rejected. For one thing, studies have shown the ineffectiveness of so-called mind-controlling techniques. Also, the high attrition rate in cults—that is, individuals who become disaffected and leave cults quite on their own—argues powerfully against the mind-control thesis. For these and other reasons, almost no one in the academic sociological community takes seriously the mind-control paradigm, though it continues to be held in the popular imagination. Part IV concludes with an examination of some common behavioral characteristics of cults—real or imagined—including authoritarianism, stripping of past associations, distortion of human sexuality, paranoia or persecution complex, and antagonism toward orthodox Christian denominations.

Part V addresses the question of why people join cults in the first place. By far the most common reason is that people have needs in their lives that are not being met and the cult holds out the promise of meeting those needs. Conversely, it is rare for people to join a cult for doctrinal reasons even though, once in it, a person may heartily embrace the group's teachings. Among the factors motivating people to join cults are the need for love and acceptance, desire for a "family," idealism, spiritual longings, and an attraction to a group's wholesome lifestyle.

Building on insights from the previous section, Part VI explores ways people can "cult-proof" their kids and their churches. While no set of techniques can offer a foolproof guarantee, there are, nevertheless, certain steps that can make cult involvement less likely. Since people join cults because of needs in their lives, the best way to keep them out of the cults is to meet those needs legitimately, through Christ. Young people are especially vulnerable because adolescence is a time of searching for an identity and for some is characterized by alienation and loneliness. Parents need to keep good lines of communication open and respect their children as individuals. They should be open and honest in living out their faith and take their children's probing questions seriously. It is also important to teach crucial principles of discernment. Cult-proofing the church is a matter of meeting members' needs so they will not feel it necessary to look elsewhere for fulfillment. Because many of the people in cults formerly had some connection with mainline Christian congregations, churches should address the intellectual, spiritual, and social needs of their members.

Printed in the USA
CPSIA information can be obtained
at www.ICGtesting.com
JSHW032117191223
54023JS00002B/5